A thought-provoking and brilliantly entertaining work of nonfiction from one of the world's leading deceivers, the creator and star of the astonishing theater show and film, *In & Of Itself*.

Derek DelGaudio always believed he was a decent, honest man. But when an old journal provides irrefutable evidence to the contrary, his memories are reawakened and Derek is forced to confront—and try to understand—his role in a significant act of deception from his past.

Using his youthful notebook entries as a road map, Derek embarks on a soulful, often funny, sometimes dark journey, retracing the path that led him to a world populated by charlatans, card cheats, and con artists. As stories are peeled away and artifices are revealed, Derek examines the mystery behind his father's vanishing act, the secret he inherited from his mother, the obsession he developed with sleight-of-hand that shaped his future, and the affinity he felt for the professional swindlers who taught him how to deceive others. And once he finds himself working as a crooked dealer in a big-money Hollywood card game, Derek begins to question his own sense of morality, and discovers that even a master of deception can find himself trapped inside an illusion.

A M O R A L M A N is a wildly engaging exploration of the fictions we live as truths. It is ultimately a book about the lies we tell ourselves and the realities we manufacture in others.

AMORALMAN

AMORALMAN

A TRUE STORY AND OTHER LIES BY

DEREK DELGAUDIO

ALFRED A. KNOPF · NEW YORK 2021

THIS IS A BORZOI BOOK
PUBLISHED BY ALFRED A. KNOPF

Copyright © 2021 by Derek DelGaudio

www.aaknopf.com

Knopf, Borzoi Books, and the colophon are registered
trademarks of Penguin Random House LLC.

Library of Congress Cataloging-in-Publication Data
Names: DelGaudio, Derek, author.
Title: Amoralman : a true story and other lies / Derek DelGaudio.
Description: New York : Alfred A Knopf, 2021.
Identifiers: LCCN 2020036299 | ISBN 9780525658559 (hardcover) |
ISBN 9780525658566 (ebook)
Subjects: LCSH: DelGaudio, Derek. | Magicians—
United States—Biography.
Classification: LCC GV1545.D45 A3 2021 | DDC 793.8092 [B]—dc23
LC record available at https://lccn.loc.gov/2020036299

Cover image: (background) KeplerDesign / Shutterstock
Cover design by John Gall

Manufactured in Canada
First Edition

For the women who made me

We are born knowing only truth. Then we see.

—ECCLESIASTES

CONTENTS

AMORALMAN

There is a cave lit by a single fire that burns high on a ledge. On the cave floor below, there are prisoners shackled from head to toe. They can't move their arms or their legs, they can't even turn their heads from side to side. All they can do is stare directly in front of them, watching the light dance on the wall.

They've never seen the outside world. The cave is their world. And all they know is what they've been shown: shadows.

The shadows tell simple stories: The shadow of a man carries the shadow of a sword. The shadow of a woman nurses the shadow of a baby. The shadow of a dog eats the shadow of an apple. It is a crude form of shadow-puppet theater.

Behind the prisoners is a man-made, freestanding wall. Hiding behind that wall is the person casting the shadows: the puppeteer. He carves little sculptures, replicating people, animals, objects, etc. He then attaches those carved objects to sticks and holds them high above his head, extending the sculptures above the wall and into the fire's light, casting the shadows onto the wall to tell a story.

But the prisoners don't know it's just a story. They do not recognize shadows as shadows. To them, the shadows are truth. They even believe that they themselves are shadows.

To pass the time, the prisoners play a "game," guessing which shadow will appear next. The prisoner who guesses correctly wins. The other prisoners praise the winner, using words like "clever" and "master of nature."

One day, a prisoner is released (breaks free?) from his shackles. He discovers the wall behind him. The puppeteer is gone. The prisoner finds the little sculptures attached to sticks and begins piecing together the ruse. He realizes that the shadows he'd seen were not real. Then the prisoner sees a small beam of light. He makes his way out of the cave and sees the world as it really is. He sees a real bird in a real tree, near a real lake. He peers into the lake and, for the first time, sees his own form. Then he looks up and stares into the sun, which blinds him.

The escapee staggers back into the dark cave and describes what he's seen, rambling about chains, and puppets, and a light in the sky. He wants to release the other prisoners, but they refuse. To them, he's a lunatic who has blinded himself. Instead of letting him release them from their bindings, the prisoners threaten to kill him, fearing they, too, would go mad.

THE OPPOSITE OF LIGHT

It was 3:00 a.m. Seated directly across from me was a brutish Armenian with a bad habit of scratching the stubble on the side of his head whenever he held a decent hand. The disgruntled look on his face had everything to do with the puny stack of poker chips in front of him. The rest of his chips, along with the chips of six other opponents who had been vanquished, were piled high in front of the only other player remaining at the table, an older man with silver hair and skin so red it looked hot to the touch. He was seated to my left and puffing on his third cigar of the evening. This is the man who had arranged the game. He was the man who had hired me to deal.

The game was held in a back room on the ground floor of a

Beverly Hills mansion. Every week, poker players from all walks
of life flocked to that house looking for serious action. The initial buy-in was ten thousand dollars, but guests were welcome to
lose as much as they'd like.

I call it a "game," but that's not really accurate. Games involve
luck and skill. You can win a game because the end is unwritten.
But at that poker table, at my table, the outcome was decided
before anyone even sat down. It was my job to decide it.

There are various words to describe my role: *Cheater* is a
broad but appropriate term. *Card mechanic*, or simply *mechanic*,
would apply. *Cardsharp* and *cardshark* are interchangeable, both
suitable. However, the precise, most accurate title is *bust-out
dealer*; I was a card mechanic secretly hired by the house[*] to pose
as a professional dealer and cheat its customers. I made sure they
went bust.

On this particular occasion, I was having trouble finishing
what we had started several hours earlier. My boss, who was
going to be the big winner that night, was annoyed that it was
taking so long to collect. What he didn't know, what I didn't
have a chance to communicate to him, was *why* it was taking so
long: The Armenian wouldn't stop staring at my hands.

Plenty of guys had stared at my hands before. That's just part
of the hell of being a card cheat: You can never know why someone is watching you intently or what they are seeing. *Is he onto*

---

[*] *House*—refers to the people or organization running and financing various
forms of gambling games.

me or just lost in thought? What did he see? What does he know? Why won't he look away?

I learned to suppress such unhelpful voices in my head. Anytime someone studied me as I shuffled or dealt, and I'd feel the fear start to creep in, I'd remind myself what my boss told me: *These people are addicts and you're their dealer. If they are staring at your hands, it's not because they think you are cheating, it's because they are waiting for their next fix.*

That private affirmation wasn't working as the Armenian stared at my hands. It felt too risky to move under fire,* so I dealt another hand on the square,† thinking that would put him at ease. But it didn't help. He just kept staring, and I grew increasingly uncomfortable.

Unfortunately, I wasn't hired to play it safe. While the Armenian was staring at my hands, my boss was giving me the universal look of "Hurry the fuck up and cheat already!" I understood his frustration. The night was getting away from us. I was tired. I couldn't tell if my eyes were dry from the smoke in the air or because I hadn't blinked since the sun had gone down.

Not to mention, my hands were so cold it hurt to shuffle cards. It wasn't the temperature in the room that was the problem, nor was it the events of this particular night; my hands were always freezing in that house. It had affected my ability to focus so I looked into it and discovered: Cold hands are the result of

---

* *Move under fire*—to use sleight-of-hand while others are watching.

† *Deal on the square*—when a cheater deals cards without cheating.

the body's fight-or-flight response. When the mind perceives a threat, adrenaline is released, increasing the heart rate and shuttling blood to the vital areas of the body. One of the first places that loses blood is the hand; as the blood leaves it takes its warmth with it. Cold hands were my body's way of telling me to flee.

I could have walked away from the table, claimed I needed a break or that I wasn't feeling well. But I had too much to prove. I *needed* to end it. Not for the money, though it was my only means of income. And not to please my boss, a man who had recently taken me under his wing. I had to know if I was worth a damn.

So I ignored the Armenian's gaze and focused on my task. I took a deep breath and, simulating the actions of shuffling and cutting the cards, I secretly arranged a good hand for the Armenian and a slightly better hand for my boss, while the Armenian said nothing and continued to stare. I exhaled with the final false cut, then sailed two cards to each of the players.

The Armenian slowly, almost skeptically, shifted his focus from my hands to peek at the cards he was just dealt. I didn't know I was in the clear until I saw him reach up and scratch the stubble on the side of his head.

My boss knew it was over, but he enjoyed toying with people, similar to the way a cat plays with its prey before killing it. The two men bet cautiously through the flop[*] and the turn.[†] The

---

[*] *Flop*—the first three of five community cards, dealt faceup in the middle of the table in a game of hold'em poker.

[†] *Turn*—the fourth community card dealt.

river* came and the Armenian said, "All in," not even bothering to shove his small stack of chips toward the center.

After some overdramatic hemming and hawing, my boss said, "Call." Both men rolled their cards over. The Armenian had two pair, Queens and Tens. My boss smiled with the cigar between his teeth and showed his three Jacks. I pulled the stack of chips away from the Armenian and scooted them toward the winner, who immediately began gleefully sorting his winnings.

The Armenian sat there, expressionless and silent. Normally when players take a beating like that they bitch and moan, or make a joke to ease the pain, or just get up and leave. But the Armenian simply sat there staring blankly at the spot on the table where his money used to be.

I ignored the awkwardness and began gathering up the cards, preparing to leave the table. But I stopped moving completely when the Armenian calmly reached behind his back and produced a snub-nosed revolver. He rested the gun on the table with his hand wrapped firmly around the handle and the barrel pointed in my direction.

The room fell deadly quiet. Even the ceiling fan, which normally hummed rhythmically, was spinning silently. If my life flashed before my eyes, it happened so quickly I didn't notice. The Armenian looked up at me and then over at my boss. Then he said, "How much can I get for this?"

We said nothing as he shoved the gun to the center and said, "Somebody gimme five hundred for it." The oxygen slowly

* *River*—the fifth and final community card in the game.

poured back into the room as the brute continued to negotiate against himself, saying, "Gimme four hundred. Come on, it's worth twice that."

Realizing he was talking to me, I stammered, "I'm not authorized to do that, sir." Then I looked at my boss, who was still stunned by the event. After a moment he, too, snapped back to reality and did the only thing he could do. He bought the pistol.

The Armenian slid the gun over to my boss in exchange for poker chips.

We took it all back the very next hand.

I was twenty-five years old when I worked as a bust-out dealer. It was a brief chapter in my life, less than six months, but it was the education of a lifetime. More importantly, I saw something extraordinary in that house.

It wasn't a vision, per se. Although it did offer me insight into my past, present, and future. And I wouldn't describe it as an out-of-body experience, but I am closer to understanding what others mean when they say that. The best way to briefly describe the experience itself is to say I lost sight of reality just enough to glimpse the truth.

After I walked away from that life, I never spoke of the incident. And I rarely spoke about my time in that house. Sharing was counter to my instincts, which were to conceal and obfuscate; these were talents I had honed as a boy and later perfected.

Also, I didn't know the legal ramifications of speaking about working as a cheater. Had I been caught cheating, not by the players but by the authorities, the charges would have included theft, illegal gambling, and conspiracy to commit fraud. I wasn't keen on the idea of inviting unnecessary trouble into my life.

"Trouble" included possible retaliation from the players themselves. Some of the marks were legitimately villainous and, as I had learned, prone to violence. As far as I know, none of them were aware that they had been cheated. Revealing that information in a public forum certainly seemed like a way of adding insult to injury.

Above all, I feared the moral implications. I had convinced myself, and the world, that I was an honest man leading a moral life. My choice to sit at that card table and steal money from strangers served as evidence to the contrary. *Why admit to deception and destroy a truth?*

Then the right friend encouraged me to write about it. It was the permission I couldn't give myself. I purchased a new journal and got to work. I was going to write a book and decided to start with the story about the Armenian. I wrote four sentences and quit on the fifth. And I didn't just stop writing that story, I abandoned the project altogether. Rather than authoring my first book, I filled the notebook with brief, random (often illegible) thoughts and crudely drawn sketches. Once full, I stuffed that notebook into a shoebox, alongside a dozen other retired journals, some dating back to high school. That shoebox then found its way into the back of a closet, where it remained for nearly a decade.

I *rediscovered* that shoebox in a recent move from Los Angeles to New York. It was like stumbling upon a time capsule I never intended to create for myself. I took a break from unpacking, sat on a stepladder, and traveled down memory lane.

The page with the Armenian incident stopped me in my tracks. But it wasn't the unfinished passage that caused me to take pause. It's what I had written below. Bolded with three exclamation marks. The words: *THE OPPOSITE OF LIGHT.*

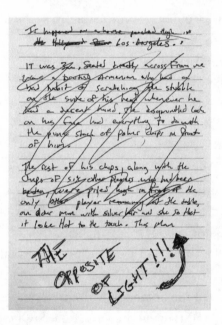

Those words were a reference to the only other time in my life I can recall stealing from another soul:

I was eleven, riding in the passenger seat of my mother's truck. She pulled over at a gas station and handed me a twenty-dollar bill. Somehow my mother had me convinced that filling the car up with gas was a rite of passage for kids in Colorado. Now I can see it was just a clever way for her to stay in the warm car.

After filling the tank, I went inside to pay the attendant. I handed him the twenty and he gave me the change: a five-dollar bill and some coins. I placed the money in my pocket, hopped back into the car, and we hit the road again.

After about ten minutes of idle chat, my mother suddenly remembered something I'd hoped she had forgotten, asking, "Hey, was there any change back there?"

I reached into my pocket and grabbed only the coins, leaving the five behind. She saw the few measly coins in my hand, said, "You can keep that," then steered us back to our discussion.

When I returned the coins to my pocket, where they joined the unseen five-dollar bill, I felt like I had gotten away with the heist of the century. The hard part was done; all that was left was to sit back and play it cool.

Before that moment, I had never stolen money from my mother. Or anyone, for that matter. I'd never shoplifted or even taken a toy from another child. I was an honest boy. A good boy. But in that moment, for some reason, I wanted that five-dollar bill. At least I thought that's what I wanted.

But as my mother continued to speak, the thrill of the swindle subsided. Her voice faded into the background and the little voice in my head began to interrogate me:

What are you doing? Why would you do that? Why didn't you show her the five?!

My eleven-year-old self had no reasonable answer to justify my actions. I didn't need the money. If I *had* needed the money, my mother would have simply given it to me. And even if I *didn't* need it, had I asked, she still would have given it to me.

Not more than five minutes passed before I crumbled under the self-imposed pressure. "Mom," I blurted out, "there's something I have to tell you." Then I sheepishly removed the five-dollar bill from my pocket, saying, "There was more change."

My mother, trying to keep her eyes on the road, glanced over at the crumpled five. She said nothing as her eyes returned to the road. I assumed she was formulating a punishment that fit the crime. After a moment of uncomfortable silence she said, "Thank you for being honest . . . You can keep that."

It was a trap. *Had to be.* I kept the bill extended toward her.

"It's yours," my mother said, nodding at the bill, "but only because you told the truth. I want you to know you can always be honest with me. Okay?"

I said, "Okay," and reluctantly placed the five in my pocket.

We sat in silence. She searched for her next words as if they were printed on the road ahead and eventually found them, saying, *"There's a lot of darkness in this world, kiddo . . . Be the light."*

THE ORIGIN OF A LIE

Back in the late '60s, on Long Island, a man named George discovered that the neighborhood hardware store he had managed for the last three years was actually owned by the Mob and they were using it to launder money. After making this discovery, George, a former naval officer, grew increasingly uncomfortable with his unintentional involvement in a criminal enterprise. When his employers started asking him to run errands, to take envelopes from here to there, he gave his two weeks' notice. In response, his employers threatened him and his family. George packed the station wagon and fled to Los Angeles to start a new life with his wife, his two older daughters, and his new baby girl, Kim.

From the moment she was born, Kim knew only chaos. Her

mother, George's wife, was a cruel drunk whose shrill voice set the loud and violent tone for the household. Kim and her sisters hung out at the beach long after the sun went down, to avoid going home. Eventually their father, too, grew weary of his wife's abuse. Kim never blamed him for leaving.

Rebelling against her mother, Kim became kind and reserved. She was a gangly girl with long hair bleached blond by the sun. By age sixteen, Kim towered above her peers at nearly six feet tall. Despite her imposing stature, she felt invisible. That's what drew her to my father. Years later she told me, "He was the first boy who ever paid attention to me."

They met in a small mountain town in California. Dad was a good-looking kid with dark hair and olive skin. He spotted Kim in the lobby of a ski lodge and struck up a conversation. They chatted for a bit, exchanged numbers, and a few weeks later they went on their first and only date.

Nine months later I was born.

My father was a rich kid from Beverly Hills. His parents didn't approve of my mother. As far as they were concerned, she was a girl from the wrong side of the tracks, and they were not about to let one mistake destroy their son's promising future.

I imagine my father, a college student, sitting on his bed. He's staring at the phone and the weight of the world is on his shoulders. Downstairs his mother, normally a model of grace, is smoking a cigarette and frantically pacing. His father, a mattress mogul, who made millions selling overpriced beds to hospitals, is sitting in his favorite leather chair nursing a glass of scotch. They have just told my father to call my sixteen-year-old mother and tell her exactly what they discussed. My father rehearses his lines:

I have my whole life ahead of me. And while you are entitled to have the baby, I cannot allow your choice to ruin the rest of my life. So I'm calling to tell you I will have no part in the child's life. This is the last time we will speak. Please do not contact me again.

I don't know how long he sat there by the phone, but I'm certain making that call and saying those words to my sweet, young, confused, vulnerable mother was the most difficult thing my father ever had to do.

Or at least it would have been, had he called. But he didn't. And while I'd like to think my father *wanted* to call, the truth is he couldn't even find enough courage to be a coward. Instead, my mother heard through the grapevine that his parents had shipped him off to another state, far from her and her mistake.

My pregnant mother was living in a cramped apartment with her alcoholic mother, who survived solely on welfare and child support. My grandmother suggested her daughter, my mother, have an abortion. Considering the circumstances, that was arguably the most thoughtful advice my grandma had ever given her daughter.

By this time my mother's father, George, had started a new family with his secretary-turned-wife. When Mom told George she was going to have a baby, he mustered up all the compassion he could to say, "You've ruined your life." To this day, my mother has never heard him utter the words "I love you."

After I was born, Mom's priority was getting us out from under Grandma's roof. A wise decision on her part. The few memories I have of my grandmother include the time she came home on the back of a motorcycle, holding a half-empty bottle of wine; the time her new "boyfriend" showed me his Hitler Youth knife; and her casual use of the N-word.

Mom dropped out of high school and got a job stocking shelves at a health-food store. Her two older sisters had their own apartments and we couch-surfed between them until Mom could afford a place of our own. She found an old laundry room that had been converted into living space. It was a single room with brick walls and a concrete floor. It had a toilet and a sink, but no kitchen.

We used a camping stove to cook our meals. Mom would clear an area on the floor and screw the gas can into the burner. I had the important job of making sure a gust of wind from outside didn't sneak by and blow the flame out before it reached the stove. I took great pride in my work.

One day my mother hesitated before striking the match. She asked me, "Do you want to know how this works?" After I nodded, she explained that the match was made out of various chemicals, and how striking the match on the box created friction, which ignited the chemicals using the oxygen in the air as fuel. Somehow, my mother had gotten her GED and was going to school to become a firefighter.

We didn't have much, but it felt like enough. *I* felt like enough. Then I watched another boy fly.

I was five, my mother was teaching me how to swim at a public pool. I wore floaties around my biceps and my mother held me on the surface of the water yelling, "Kick! Kick!"

In the center of the pool I saw a little boy standing on his father's shoulders, while the mother cheered them on. The father and son counted to three. On three, the dad propelled the boy into the air. The boy rocketed into the sky, defying gravity, flying so high that he touched the clouds. Eventually the boy returned from the heavens, crashing into the water, and emerged with a smile as his mother and father laughed in delight.

We got out of the pool and, as Mom dried me off, I asked her, "Where's my dad?"

"I don't know, kiddo."

Not long after, Mom started dating Ken, a man with broad shoulders and a caterpillar mustache. He took us camping. It was my first time outside of the city. I eagerly helped Ken set up the tent and collect firewood. He showed me how to bait a hook, and I sat next to him as he fished. Most kindergartners wouldn't have sat so patiently for so long.

The next day, I became violently ill and our serene excursion came to an abrupt end. We packed up the car and drove back to the city, where my mother nursed me back to health in our tiny apartment. There wasn't enough room for Ken, so he left. We never saw him again.

Later that year, when I was six years old, my mother moved us to a slightly larger apartment in the same building, on the second floor. It had a kitchen, so we didn't have to cook our meals like campers. It also had a separate bedroom, which allowed for more privacy. I'd fall asleep on the bed. When my mother was ready to go to sleep, she'd make room for herself, picking me up and moving me to the cot next to the bed.

One night I was tossing and turning, trying to fall asleep, while my mother was in the living room. I was afraid of being alone in the dark, so she always left our bedroom door cracked, allowing in enough light to keep the boogeyman away. It was past my bedtime and I should've been sound asleep. But I was thirsty. So I got out of bed and crept toward the kitchen to get a cup of water.

I had expected to see my mother seated on the couch watching TV. What I did not expect was the stranger seated next to her. I just stood there in my Ninja Turtles pajamas, watching, trying to understand why my mother was passionately kissing another woman.

After a few seconds, my mother noticed me and bolted off the couch as if *I* were the parent interrupting her teenage make-out session. Flustered, she moved toward me, saying, "Hey, kiddo, is the TV too loud? What's up?"

My eyes were transfixed on the boyish lady on the couch. She was a few years older than my mom, with a face full of freckles and a mullet. I remember staring at the image on her white T-shirt: two women standing in profile, one embracing the other from behind, both shirtless, their breasts concealed by their embrace. The women were looking over their shoulders, staring directly at me.

Earlier that year, my mother had already taught me the meaning of the word "gay." I didn't know it at the time, but she was arming me with the vocabulary I'd need for a difficult discussion.

I asked her, "Are you gay?"

She said, "Yes," and I began to cry.

When she asked me why I was crying, I replied, "I don't want you to be gay."

She began to weep. I reached out to hug her and she pulled me onto her lap, where we cried together. After the tears subsided, my mother loosened her embrace and got me a glass of water. I took a long sip and stared down the lady near me on the couch.

The butch woman broke her silence, saying, "Hi! I'm Jill. Those are cool pajamas! Are those turtles?"

I explained, "The blue is Leonardo. Donatello is purple. Michelangelo is orange. Raphael is red and he's my favorite."

The three of us continued to make small talk. My mom cracked a few jokes, we had a few gentle laughs. Then my mother asked me if I was ready to go to bed. When I told her I was, she took me by the hand and I waved good night to the lady on the couch.

As Mom tucked me in, I asked, "When did you turn gay?"

She replied, "I've always been gay, I just didn't know it."

When my mother was four years old, all she wanted for her birthday was the Roy Rogers Cowboy Adventure Set. The box contained a six-shooter and holster, a silver deputy badge, a cowboy hat, and spurs. Instead, her mother bought her the Dale Evans (Roy's wife) cowgirl set. It had a pink vest, a sparkly hat, and a dainty lasso. Mom put on that costume and grew up feeling like she never took it off.

She spent the first two decades of her life believing she was straight. She didn't *choose* to believe that fiction. It was inevitable. Every depiction of life—every book, every TV show, the ads between the shows—her friends, even her family, told her that same exact story. How could she not believe the only thing she ever knew?

Then, when she was twenty-two, while training to become an EMT, she met a loving couple: Sheri and Sandra. Meeting these two women—seeing them living their authentic lives—unlocked a truth that had been buried deep within my mother. She recognized that she had mistaken role-playing for real life. No more pink vests or sparkly hats. She was done playing the part she was handed.

The moment she realized she had been living in the proverbial closet, she kicked the door down with a pair of steel-toed Doc Martens. She told her parents who she really was, choosing her freedom over their love. Then she hopped into a Jeep and drove off into the sunset, waving a pride flag, singing along with Melissa Etheridge.

She refused to live silently, shamefully, or fearfully in the shadow of a secret. With one small exception. She didn't know how to tell her son, whom she loved more than life itself. When I stumbled in on her make-out session with Jill, I had unknowingly—and uncomprehendingly—relieved her of her last shred of secrecy.

Mom tucked me into bed that night and assured me, "Nothing has changed, sweetie. I still love you more than anything in the world." Then, hoping I'd reassure her, she asked, "You know that, right?"

I knew she loved me, so I said, "Yes." But everything had changed. When I said, "I love you, too," her eyes welled with tears. Then she kissed me on my forehead and left the room. When she closed the door, I didn't bother reminding her to leave it cracked. The moment the room went dark, I buried my face into my pillow and began to weep.

I wasn't crying because she was gay. I was mourning the loss of the father I'd never have. I fell asleep knowing I'd never fly.

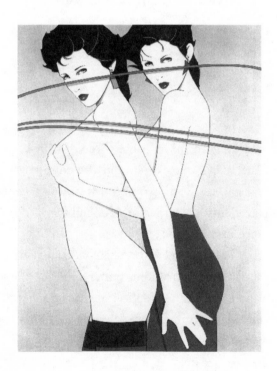

WHERE VANISHED THINGS GO

Mom shacked up with Jill, and the three of us moved to Colorado. Only a few fire departments in the country were hiring, and even fewer were hiring women. Mom was accepted to the firefighting academy in Denver and looked forward to landing a job somewhere in the state.

Jill was tough. She had a life-isn't-fair-so-deal-with-it attitude, something she inherited from her father while herding cattle on the family ranch. I never needed to imagine how hard life might have been for a lesbian in the middle of Oklahoma because Jill made sure to tell me, often. Any pain I felt, or struggle I had, was measured against her own.

Our two-bedroom apartment was located on the outskirts of Denver. The ceilings looked like popcorn and the floors gave me splinters. The place was furnished and decorated with Jill's stuff. Her furniture had sharp corners and shiny surfaces. Glass-blown dolphins were scattered all over the place. Each wall had a different Patrick Nagel poster, like the print on her T-shirt, images of colorless women with jet-black hair and rich red lips, voguing in various poses. And there was a futuristic CD player that opened when you waved your hand in front of it, which I was strictly forbidden to play with.

The apartment complex had its own jungle gym and swing set, and my mom would let me play there, watching me from our living room window, giving me a sense of freedom.

That's where I met Ryan, a lanky eight-year-old with spiky blond hair, who lived on the second floor. He was a boy's boy. He liked wrestling in the mud and wanted to be the first profes-sional football player/dirt bike racer. But more than anything, he loved Jesus.

"Who's Jesus?" I asked.

"You don't know who Jesus is?"

I admitted I had never heard of him. Ryan was astonished by my ignorance. After he got over the initial shock, he told me all about the Son of God.

That night I went home and asked Mom why I hadn't heard of this Jesus fellow. She did her best to explain the concept of religion and spirituality. And how different people believed dif-ferent things.

When Ryan invited me to attend church with his family, my mother went downstairs to meet Ryan's parents, who were always so nice and polite. That Sunday, my mother put me in my nicest clothes, a pair of white pants and a blue shirt with stripes, and I went to church for the very first time.

We took our seats in a large auditorium; there must have been a few hundred people there. Music played. Everyone started singing and clapping. Then a storyteller in a suit walked onstage holding a book, which he occasionally slapped to emphasize the name "Jesus!"

At one point the storyteller told everyone to close their eyes. I kept mine open, certain that others would disobey the command. But everyone else did as they were told. And when their eyes were closed, they all had the same pleasant look on their faces, as if they were all looking at the same lovely thing. I closed my eyes to try to see what they were seeing.

Then music began playing again and I heard someone say, "You can open your eyes now." I stood there while everyone sang along. In the lobby we ate cookies and had lemonade. Everyone there was so nice and smiley.

I went home and told Mom, "I want to be a Christian."

She suggested we look at other religions before I made that decision. I agreed, but told her that, in the meantime, I wanted to go back to church. She said, "Fine," and the next week I returned to hear more stories, listen to more music, eat cookies and drink lemonade. It was hard to understand why anyone *wouldn't* want to be a Christian.

I continued attending church with Ryan's family, and I started eating dinner at his place on Wednesdays. Every meal was a feast, with creamy mashed potatoes and butter biscuits; even the green beans were good. I didn't know I could like green beans. Before eating, we always had to say grace:

> *God is great,*
> *God is good,*
> *and we thank Him for our food.*
> *By His hand*
> *we are fed,*
> *Give us, Lord,*
> *our daily bread.*
> *Amen.*

One night, Ryan and I were eating our pie and ice cream on his balcony, and he asked me, "Who's that woman living with you?"

"That's my *other* mom," I told him.

He looked confused by my response. The same look I had when I heard the name "Jesus" for the first time. I enlightened him, saying, "Some people have a mommy and a daddy. I have two mommies."

He nodded as if he understood and we finished our ice cream.

The next day, when I saw Ryan on the playground, he hopped off the swing and ran in the other direction. Then he didn't come to get me for dinner on Wednesday night. I went a week without seeing him, which is an eternity when you're seven.

I finally caught him on the stairwell and asked him where he had been.

He replied, "I can't be your friend anymore."

When I asked him why, he told me, "It's a sin to be gay."

I didn't know what "sin" meant.

He cut to the chase, telling me, "Your mother is going to hell," the dreadful place I had learned about at church.

I went home in tears. Becoming a Christian meant abandoning my mother, if not in this life, then in the next. I could never do that. Which meant not only was she going to hell but I was going with her.

My mother assured me that neither of us was going to hell. She also told me how wrong it was for Ryan to say that to me. Then she went downstairs and gave Ryan's parents an earful. I didn't hear what she said but I saw how angry she was when she headed out the door. And how angry she still was when she got back.

The next day, at school, I sensed something was different. Outside my classroom, I saw Ryan huddled with other kids from my class. He wasn't even in the same grade as me; there was no reason for him to be there. When he saw me approaching, he walked the other way. As I passed by my classmates they snickered and pointed. Yesterday I was just another kid. Now I was the freak with two moms.

It turned out our neighborhood was composed of two different religious groups: conservative Christians, and *ultraconservative* Christians. Ryan and his family were members of the latter. The church they had been taking me to was New Life Church, whose congregants used their spare time to block entrances to abortion clinics and protest gay pride marches.

The next thing I knew, a Bible with Leviticus 18 bookmarked appeared on our doorstep. Not long after, the word *FAGGOT* materialized on the back of my mother's car. Then the Lord's message of forgiveness was delivered in the form of a brick, thrown through our living room window.

My mother had taught me the value of truth, but she neglected to teach me the cost. She told me that honesty was always the best policy, but now I had evidence to the contrary. I told Ryan the truth about my family and it destroyed my world.

It wasn't long before we packed up the Nagel posters and glass dolphins and moved to the other side of town, giving me a fresh start at a new school. On the first day of class, Mom walked me to the bus stop. When I could see the other kids waiting at the curb, I shooed her away, telling her I'd be fine. She watched from afar as I boarded the bus with my little backpack. Once on board, I found an empty seat and hoped no one sat next to me.

In class, I nabbed a desk toward the back, where I could ob-serve the kids around me. They seemed nice enough. But Ryan had been nice. Everyone was nice. Until they weren't.

My new teacher, Mrs. Doggett, introduced herself and gave us our first assignment: "On your desk is a piece of paper. In the back of the room you'll find colored pencils and markers. We will spend the first half of class drawing family portraits. The second half, we will go around the room and, one by one, share those drawings with the class."

I had been there ten minutes and the teacher was already try-ing to expose me. The other kids passed by my desk on their way to pick up their cups of freshly sharpened pencils. I waited until they returned to their desks to get mine. Then I just sat there, staring at the blank sheet of paper. When I looked up, everyone around me had their heads down, doing exactly as they were told. Not wanting to draw attention, I forced myself to pick up a pencil, and I began to draw.

I started by drawing a horizontal line. Then a tree and the sun above it, with a few clouds. I put some V-shaped birds in the air. Then I drew myself. I drew my mother. And that's it. I imagined it was a portrait of my family playing hide-and-go-seek and Jill was hiding behind the tree.

We presented our drawings, one by one. The teacher called on us alphabetically. I felt my hands turn cold when the first name was called. Before I knew it, I was in front of the class, displaying my drawing. I told the class, "This is me and this is my mom." The teacher tried to get me to elaborate, but I didn't have more to say.

I got a gold star for that drawing, but the work never made it home to be pinned on the fridge. I knew my mother's feelings would be hurt by the glaring omission. Sacrificing accolades would become routine. I'd rather be safe than praised.

As time went on, the lurking danger at school slowly revealed itself. At recess the kids tackled each other on the yard, playing the game they called "Smear the Queer." In the halls, kids hurled the word "faggot" at the weaklings. And the teachers let them.

It took months before I made a friend, Mike, a Korean boy. I'd go over to his house and jump on his trampoline. We'd toss a football around and help (i.e., watch) his stepdad, a car mechanic, fix up the old Mustang they had in their backyard. Mike had video games and I didn't, so it made sense that we spent time at his place. Or at least that was the excuse I had for not having him come to my house.

Eventually I had to have him over. I made sure Jill wasn't home. Then, before I let him enter, I ran inside, hid our family photos, and took down the rainbow flag that was on a pole attached to the house in back. Thankfully, Mike thought I lacked sufficient amenities and games to keep us entertained. I was grateful when he suggested we go back to hang out at his place, where his mom, the attractive flight attendant, was ordering pizza.

After a year of friendship, he spotted "the other lady" and asked me the dreaded question: "Who's that?"

I replied with a truth that concealed another. "That's my mom's roommate."

My mother had given me that answer. "Roommate" was a word, I later learned, she used only in my presence, for my benefit. Never once was she ashamed of who she was or afraid of others. She just wanted me to feel safe, so she provided me with the armor I needed to face the world.

At school, I kept a low profile and, with the exception of Mike, continued to render myself invisible. I managed to stay out of trouble until one incident that occurred in the fourth grade.

Every morning, before class started, we children stood by our desks, placed our hands where we thought our hearts were, and recited:

I pledge allegiance
to the Flag
of the United States of America,
and to the Republic
for which it stands,
one Nation
under God,
indivisible,
with liberty
and justice for all.

One morning, I didn't speak or stand. When the teacher didn't say anything, I repeated the protest the following day. This time the teacher noticed me and told me to rise; I remained seated. After the pledge I got into a brief argument with the teacher, resulting in my first trip to the principal's office.

The principal interrogated me, trying to understand what sparked the protest. I told him I didn't want to pledge my allegiance, but refused to explain why. I couldn't, not to him, not even when my mother arrived and tried to coax it out of me.

The moment my mother and I got into her car to head home, I explained what I couldn't risk telling the other adults. There were two reasons for my silent protest. The first was the line "liberty and justice for all."

"That's not true, it's a lie," I told my mother.

"What do you mean?"

I explained my reasoning: Earlier that year, Jill had been in a car accident coming home from work. My mother rushed to the hospital with me in tow. But when we got there, we were not permitted to see Jill. I watched my mother beg and plead with doctors and nurses, "Please let me see my wife," but the staff refused. In the eyes of the law, my mom and Jill were not married. We had to wait in the lobby until sunrise, when normal visiting hours began. I didn't particularly get along with Jill, but even I knew this was unfair. And needlessly cruel.

Sitting next to my mother in the car, I continued justifying my protest, telling her about the other line in the Pledge of Allegiance that sparked my dissent, "one Nation under God." I had sung God's praises before, calling him "good" and "great," even thanking him. And for what? He had already caused me so much pain. And if he was so great, why were his followers a constant source of terror? I saw no reason to stand up for that son of a bitch.

To my surprise, instead of reprimanding me for disobeying the authorities, my mother said she was proud of me. She told me she supported my decision. The next day she drove me to school early, went in, and spoke to the principal on her own. A compromise was struck: I could remain silent and I didn't have to place my hand over my heart, but I had to stand. It was a fair deal.

Over the next few years, I continued to quietly underachieve. Every parent-teacher conference was the same. Some version of: "He's a bright kid but he's not applying himself. If he doesn't do something about his grades, he'll be held back a year." I always managed to get my act together enough to pass and avoid summer school. But just barely.

Only once can I recall enjoying what school had to offer. It was a homework assignment given to our fifth-grade class: Write about your favorite movie. For the first time, my interests were aligned with my education.

Since I could remember, I had often sought refuge in films. We had a small TV that had a built-in VHS player, and I watched movies as often as Mom would allow. I gravitated toward the humorous and whimsical, I suppose because my life was neither. I escaped into *The Princess Bride*, particularly fond of Inigo Montoya. I developed an inexplicable obsession with Charlie Chaplin; all I wanted for Christmas was the VHS box set containing the Tramp's greatest hits. I adored Steve Martin, especially in *Dirty Rotten Scoundrels*. But the film that towered above all others for me at age eleven was *Willy Wonka & the Chocolate Factory*, starring Gene Wilder. That's what I chose to write about.

The teacher was very clear about the assignment, reiterating several times, "Don't just tell me about the movie, tell me *why* you like it so much." Uncharacteristically, I took the assignment seriously. I even did research, reading interviews with the actors and filmmakers, and seeking out behind-the-scenes footage.

In the essay, I drew parallels between me and Charlie, the fatherless youth looking to escape his meager existence. I praised Willy Wonka for the wondrous world he had built for himself and the lengths he went to protect it. I wrote about the importance of the gobstopper, how it was a test of decency and integrity, and how doing the right thing, even when it was hard, was the key to getting what you ultimately want.

There is one specific detail from that paper that stands out in my memory because it's something I have carried with me to this very day. It's an anecdote, not from the movie, but something that occurred prior to filming. Upon reading the script, Gene Wilder told Mel Stuart, the director, he'd take the role under one condition: When the audience first sees Wonka, Wilder wanted him to have a cane and a severe limp. Then, as Wonka feebly walks toward the crowd, his cane gets stuck in a brick, at which point he begins to fall. At the last moment, he does a forward summersault, springing to his feet, and the crowd applauds.

The befuddled director asked, "Why do you want to do that?"

Wilder replied, "Because from that time on, no one will know if I'm lying or telling the truth."

That essay was the first A-plus I had ever received. The grade was seen as a potential turning point, a shining example of the academic abilities I had previously chosen not to apply. My mother and teacher thought I might finally become the student they believed I could and should be. But that excellence was an anomaly; the hope I had given them was false. I resumed limping along at school.

I developed a general melancholy, which worsened with time. The day I had drawn my family portrait, the one with Jill hiding behind the tree, I had created a secret. Keeping that secret was a relentless and exhausting endeavor. I found it difficult to wake up most mornings. When I'd sleep through my alarm, my mother would burst in, belting a song I had never heard on any radio station:

Good morning starshine
The earth says hello
You twinkle above us
We twinkle below . . .

She was a terrible singer, but she knew that, so she played it for laughs. When I refused to get up, keeping the blanket pulled over my head, she'd tug on my toes until they cracked. I'd squirm, and the annoyance would inevitably be enough to get me out of bed. And once I was up, she was desperate to see me smile. But I was too tired to smile.

One day, shortly after my twelfth birthday, I picked a Coke can up off the kitchen counter and it exploded like a firecracker. It scared the shit out of me. I looked at the counter and saw a little spring-loaded device, like a mousetrap, but instead of cheese there was a cap from a cap gun. Even though it almost scared me to death, I thought it was hilarious.

Before that, my mother had never played a practical joke on me. But it had been several months since we had laughed together, and desperate times called for desperate measures. I asked her where she got the gag. She said there was a joke shop near her firehouse. Until that moment I thought only adults owned stores; clearly this was the work of some sort of diabolical child genius. I demanded to go at once.

Unfortunately, my mother's firehouse was eighty miles from our apartment, in a relatively small but majestic mountain town, Colorado Springs. Or, as the locals called it, "the Springs." Depending on the snow, her commute would take between two and four hours, each way. The last thing she wanted to do was go there on her day off.

Luckily for me, my mother's health insurance was covered by the city, which meant I could only see doctors in the Springs. And wouldn't you know it, I was due for my annual trip to the dentist. I had never been so excited to have my teeth cleaned.

After months of dreaming about the joke shop, the day finally came. The entire car ride there I imagined the mischievous wonders that awaited me. I pictured an epic warehouse, full of ingenious pranks, whose clientele consisted of everyone from Wile E. Coyote to Groucho Marx.

The store was at the end of a long brick building. Mom wanted to grab a coffee before we went in, but I couldn't wait a second longer. She told me she'd meet me in there and I didn't hesitate to run ahead. The bell above the door clanged as I entered. The floor creaked with every step. It wasn't nearly as large as I had envisioned. But it certainly was a visual feast.

Feather boas, like the ones I had seen in movies I wasn't supposed to have watched, hung from a pipe on the ceiling. Rubber monster masks wrapped around the perimeter where the walls met the ceiling. A display of outlandish sunglasses stood next to a rack of Mardi Gras beads. There was a display of makeup that was used to create realistic bruises and cuts. An entire wall devoted to fake teeth. Wigs in every imaginable shape and color, and hats that spanned from gangster-type fedoras to Viking helmets.

I spotted the arrow-through-the-head gag I had seen Steve Martin wear on TV. Then I heard a voice say, "Hello, young man. Can I help you find something?" I turned to see a middle-aged man in a flannel shirt, with glasses and a thick beard, standing behind one of the glass display cases filled with unfamiliar doodads and gadgets.

I told him I was looking for the exploding can gag. He led me to a wall of practical jokes, then left me alone to fill my basket. I found the exploding gizmo and grabbed all the other essentials: shocking gum, itching powder, stink bombs, super-spicy candy, disappearing ink, and little firecrackers you could shove into cigars. I didn't know anyone who smoked cigars, but it didn't matter, I was in heaven.

I passed on the whoopee cushion, though. They offered an impressive variety, I won't deny that. But I felt the concept was a bit hackneyed and simply didn't align with the sophisticated humor I was striving to achieve.

I went to the cash register and the man leaned in to say, "Can I get your opinion on something?"

He asked as if my opinion mattered. I wasn't used to that from anyone other than my mother, but I cautiously replied, "Yes."

He reached into his pocket and removed a small black pocket-knife. The rusted blade was folded into the black handle, which was faded and scratched. It looked like it had been sitting in a gutter for a year, which made it all the more confusing that he presented it with pride.

"So what do you think?" he asked.

To spare his feelings I replied with an ambiguous, "Cool."

"Be honest," he insisted.

"It looks like a piece of junk."

"Perfect! Thank you," he said. Then he put the knife back into his pocket and went about his business.

I couldn't fathom why he was so excited about something so unextraordinary. I had an overwhelming desire to understand why he was so happy with that crappy knife. I *now* know it wasn't just a knife; it was bait.

"What's so special about that knife?" I asked.

He looked over his shoulder to make sure I was the only one who could hear him. (We were alone in the store.) Then he leaned over the counter. I leaned toward him, the pocketknife between us.

"See, I used to have a beautiful knife with a gorgeous pearl handle and shiny blade. One day I left it on the counter and someone stole it. I loved that knife so much, I spent weeks looking for another one. I didn't find the *exact* same knife, but I found one that was very close: same pearl handle, the blade was just as shiny. I wanted to make sure nobody stole *this* one. So I hid it." He looked down at the knife and said, "Here."

Confused, I asked, "Where?"

He said, "Here," again, referring again to the crummy black knife between us.

"You ruined your knife on purpose?" I asked.

"No! I just made it *look* like this so nobody takes it. Look, I'll show you."

I nodded politely and I started to walk away.

He stopped me, saying, "Look, look, I'll show you."

And show me he did. He began to gently shake the knife. Then, slowly, the rusty old black knife transformed into the shiny white knife he'd spoken of moments before.

He handed me the knife as evidence of his sanity. I inspected it, thoroughly. No rust. No muck or scratches. Not one spot of darkness on it. It was indeed beautiful.

I struggled to understand what I had just witnessed. Then I mimicked the action he used to transform the knife, shaking it as he did. Nothing changed.

"You want it to go back to black?" he said, taking it from me. Then he gave it a shake, like he did before, and the pearly white knife changed back into the crummy black knife again.

Still processing what I had just witnessed, I watched him place the folded knife in his hand and close his fingers around it. He squeezed and slowly opened his hand to reveal the knife was gone. It went to the place where vanished things go.

I stood there with my mouth open, replaying what I had just seen and heard. Then I summoned the courage to ask the question I didn't realize he was expecting. "Can you teach me how to do that?"

He replied, "Only if you can keep a secret."

EVEN SECRETS HAVE SECRETS

In the earliest notebook, the only spiral-bound one, I found an entry where I lamented the narrowness of the accepted definitions of the term *sleight-of-hand*.

MERRIAM-WEBSTER DICTIONARY: A cleverly executed trick or deception.

CAMBRIDGE DICTIONARY: Speed and skill of the hand when performing tricks.

MACMILLAN DICTIONARY: Clever and quick use of your hands, especially when performing a magic trick.

I was particularly annoyed by the fact that all of them emphasized trickery. To me these were pathetic simplifications that focused on a limited context rather than the activity itself. *I don't need to deceive someone to execute sleight-of-hand,* I wrote. I was so dissatisfied with the definitions that I created my own:

Sleight-of-hand refers to the practice of using fine motor skills and psychological principles to create unnatural events through seemingly natural actions.

I had forgotten I wrote this. When I read it, I chuckled thinking about the hubris required to define a thing that already had several credible definitions. Then I sympathized with that young man's frustration, remembering how so much of his world felt so unnatural.

My obsession began that day at the magic shop. Instead of buying practical jokes, I used the money I had saved to purchase a book on sleight-of-hand. The cover had an illustration of three cups, two balls, a conjuror's wand, and it was appropriately titled *Sleight of Hand: A Practical Manual of Legerdemain for Amateurs & Others,* by Edwin T. Sachs. That book was my bible.

My place of worship was a dusty construction site. New tract houses were being built on a wide-open plot of land in my neighborhood. Each weekday, the workers abandoned the site around four or five o'clock. Once the coast was clear, I'd park my bike behind one of the partially completed homes and enter the property through a hole where a window would someday be.

Once inside, I'd brush aside any loose nails and sit on the floor. From my backpack I'd remove the objects required for the ritual: A deck of playing cards. Four Kennedy half-dollars. A bouncy ball and marbles. A stick that I modified to stand in for a pocketknife. (By "modified" I mean I found a broken branch, then used the sidewalk to file its rough edges down until it was approximately the size of the knife the man behind the counter made vanish.) And a flashlight for when the sun went down.

I'd rest the book in my lap and teach myself the fundamental principles of legerdemain. I sat there for hours, alone and in silence, slowly translating the words on the page into actions in my hands. I did this nearly every day for an entire summer.

On the weekends there were no workers on-site, so I could go as early as I'd like. I'd wake up, make a sandwich, grab a Fruit by the Foot and a Capri Sun juice, and head to my secret lair. But I wasn't just going there for privacy. History was repeating itself; I had inherited the ritual of staying out long after the sun went down to avoid a turbulent household.

Lesbians, it seems, are not immune to the cliché of marrying their mothers. In Jill my mother had found a drunk for a partner. When the two of them bickered, I retreated to my room. When their quarrels reverberated through the thin walls of my bedroom, I put on headphones and listened to comedy albums. One night, even the headphones didn't help, so I snuck out the back window in search of a quiet place to continue studying. That's when I found my private retreat at the construction site.

The first thing I learned from my book of secrets was how to vanish a coin. The text was convoluted. I had to read each sentence several times to decipher it. "*The coin is held between the thumb and forefinger, and the latter then slid aside, so that the coin rests upon the side of the middle finger . . .*"

There *were* illustrations, but they were few and far between. It wasn't until I had worked through the entire sequence that I realized I was learning how to simulate the action of transferring a coin from one hand to another. I then practiced this action, pretending to place a coin into my hand, over and over again.

After a week, I felt confident enough to show my mother; I was ready for my first performance. Mom had just taken a shower and the bathroom door was closed. I could hear the hair dryer blowing. When I knocked, Mom shouted, "Just a minute!" I knocked again. My mother opened the door and, a little annoyed, said, "What? What is it?!"

Displaying the shiny half-dollar at my fingertips, I said, "Watch."

"Can you gimme a minute?!"

"Just look!" I said, insisting my audience pay attention.

She watched as I placed the coin into my hand, made a fist, and, with a theatrical squeeze, made the half-dollar disappear. I looked up to receive my applause and my mother bluntly said, "It's in your other hand."

I was furious she'd seen through the subterfuge. "How'd you know?!"

"I don't know, it just looked suspicious."

"What do you mean, 'suspicious'?!"

"You were holding your hand funny. Also, the way you put it in your other hand looked fishy."

I interrogated her, demanding she tell me exactly what she saw and when she saw it. She humored my obsessive questions for a bit, then she tapped out, saying, "All I know is it didn't look right, the hand you were hiding it in didn't look normal! Now let me finish drying my hair!"

What does "right" look like? What is "normal"?

I asked myself variations of these questions as I sat in front of my bedroom mirror holding the coin. Rather than pretending to place it into my hand, I *actually* placed a coin in my hand and closed my fist around it. I repeated the honest action. Then again. And again. I did this hundreds of times, each time evaluating what exactly was happening: *Where are my fingers at any given moment? How much tension am I holding and where? How fast do I move?* And on and on.

Then, after thoroughly obsessing over the *authentic* action, I simulated the act, *pretending* to place the coin into my other hand. The differences between the two actions were painfully obvious. Just as Mom said, the simulated action didn't look "right" or "normal." But now I was able to spot the glaring inconsistencies. And I began making the necessary adjustments, blurring the visible distinctions between true and false.

School started up again in the fall. After studying and practicing, uninterrupted, for months, I was frustrated that the seventh grade was now interfering with my education. Within the first week, I was reprimanded for reading my magic book in class. People didn't recognize the cover or its title, which only made them look closer. At recess, I caught a nosy kid peeking over my shoulder as I was studying with cards in hand. So I went to the library and took the dust jacket off a copy of *The Wizard of Oz*, then wrapped it around my book of secrets so I could carry it around and read it in public without drawing attention.

As I wrote in one notebook: *Even my secrets have secrets.*

Not long after, the teacher spotted me fiddling with a deck of cards during class and told me to put them away. When it happened again, she took the cards and said, "If I see you with these things again, you're going to detention."

All I heard was "If I see . . ." Challenge accepted.

I created a little game for myself. The rules were simple: If the teacher sees me practicing, I lose.

During class, I began discreetly removing cards from my pocket, concealing them in my hands, then returning them to my pocket, without anyone being the wiser. I'd take entire tests with cards secretly lodged in both palms. When the teacher glanced in my direction, I'd freeze, holding perfectly still, as if the teacher's vision were based on movement. I'd have to remind myself to "look natural."

Soon I graduated to coins, which were much riskier. A sudden slip would send the coin crashing to my desk or, worse, the floor. The quieter the moment in class, the more careful I had to be. The slightest mistake and the coin would fall, hitting the ground with a clang. Manipulating a coin during a test was like walking a high-wire without a net. While the other kids were absorbed in their seventh-grade math exams, I was focused on the death-defying feats in the palms of my hands.

Eventually I slipped. The half-dollar crashed to the floor and everyone looked. The coin rolled to the front of the room, where the teacher picked it up. She didn't know where it came from and I wasn't about to claim it was mine. I figured fifty cents was a small price to pay to avoid detention.

The next day I had a neighbor help me drill a small hole through a half-dollar, tied two inches of fishing line to it, and looped the other end around my middle finger. That way, instead of crashing to the floor, the coin would dangle for a second, then calmly—and silently—return to its proper position.

I started making notes when I couldn't covertly practice or read my book of secrets. It was yet another way of *appearing* productive and engaged. At first, I just made extensive lists of the techniques I was practicing and moves I had yet to learn. Occasionally, I daydreamed about effects (illusions) I'd someday create. And, although I probably wasn't aware of it at the time, I started connecting myself to my practice.

Occasionally a peer would notice me handling a deck of cards and ask me what I was doing. I'd claim I was just playing solitaire. If they said, "Do a trick," I'd respond, "No," because I had no interest in performing. This, I discovered, was highly unusual.

Kids who develop an interest in magic are typically drawn to the performative aspects of the craft. They enjoy performing; it's a way of getting attention and feeling special. Conjuring becomes the bridge that connects them to the world.

But I didn't want a bridge to connect to others. I wanted a fortress to keep them out. Performing would draw unnecessary attention to me *and* it would expose my interest in secrecy. If people knew I was capable of keeping secrets, they might wonder what else I was hiding; I wasn't willing to risk being exposed.

Then the first secret I ever had vanished.

I was in my room practicing when I heard a loud crash, followed by an even louder thud. I raced out of my room to discover my mother, on her hands and knees, crying, trying to salvage a photo from its broken frame. She looked up at me and said, "It's just us again, kiddo." My mother's eight-year relationship with Jill had come to its climactic end.

Mom was a single parent again. Which meant I no longer had

to worry about people asking about "the other lady." No more hiding family photos or worrying about what friends thought of the Nagel prints. Mom had long hair and wore eyeliner, which meant as long as she was single, she could, as they say, "pass." As long as she was single, she was "normal," which meant we were safe. I could relax.

But I didn't relax. I couldn't. Next to food and water, secrecy had become an essential part of my survival; secrets were shelter.

After I finished the eighth grade, we moved eighty miles south, to Colorado Springs. The Springs was known for two things: 1) a military presence, as it was home to several bases, including the North American Aerospace Defense Command (NORAD) and the Air Force Academy; and 2) having more Christians per capita than anywhere else in the country, being home to several megachurch organizations, including New Life Church *and* Focus on the Family. In essence, my mother would spend her days saving the lives of people who thought she was an abomination, surrounded by coworkers who agreed.

To my mother's surprise, I didn't object to moving again. By that time, when I was fourteen, I was used to it; we had already packed up and moved seven times. More importantly, relocating to the Springs meant only one thing to me: After nearly two years, I'd finally be able to go back to the magic shop. And living in the same city meant I could go any time I wanted.

As luck would have it, the humble two-bedroom apartment my mother found for us was four blocks from the magic shop. I helped my mother unload the moving truck as if trying to break a world speed record. She had to yell, "Stop throwing the boxes!" After I placed the last box in the room that would be mine, I bolted out the door and ran straight to the magic shop.

The bell over the door clanged and the floor still creaked, exactly as I remembered. Walter, the man with the little black pocketknife, was right where I'd left him, still behind the counter. He was always there because he owned the place. To my surprise, he looked at me and said, "Welcome back!"

For the first time in my life, I felt like I was home. I wanted to spend every waking moment at the shop. But I had to help Mom finish unpacking and settle us into our new apartment. And I only had a few days to do it; I was starting high school in less than a week. I bought two new books with the money I had saved doing chores and told Walter I'd see him soon.

You know that trope in movies, where the kid moves to the new town and attends high school, where he or she is befriended by another lovable outcast on the first day? That didn't happen to me.

Every school day was a prison sentence. The misery started at the grotesque hour of 7:00 a.m. I sat in the back of the classroom and discreetly ate breakfast, always something I had grabbed in a hurry, like a granola bar. The bell rang at the end of class, around the time I wiped the last fleck of sleep from my eyes. The next class was the same, in the sense that I had absolutely no interest in whatever the teacher was writing on the chalkboard. I wasn't *uninterested* in receiving an education; I just didn't care for the curriculum *they* offered.

The school's only redeeming feature was its proximity to the magic shop. During the lunch break, I would cut across the park where meth was openly sold, grab a less-than-nutritious meal at Taco Bell, then hustle over to the shop to eat standing at one of the glass counters. I'd converse with Walt and listen to him gab with the regular customers until the last possible second. Then I'd reluctantly return to school for the second half of the day, which was more tedious than the first.

After school, I returned to the shop, where I stayed until closing time, 9:00 p.m. I hung out there so often that—as I learned years later—my mother took Walter to coffee to make sure he wasn't a pedophile. Apparently Walt passed whatever test she had administered, because she decided that she could trust him and his wife, Maggie. On the nights Mom worked, I'd go over to Walt and Maggie's house for dinner.

Every night at home I'd lock myself in my room, reading books Walt had loaned me and practicing, usually falling asleep with a deck of cards in my hand around 2:00 a.m. The routine caught up with me. As the months passed, my grades worsened, which wasn't a surprise. What did come as a surprise were the social repercussions.

Apparently, my self-imposed isolation was seen as an act of aggression toward some of my classmates. I had completely alienated myself from my peers. The atmosphere at school became hostile.

The first stone was cast while my class was walking from the classroom to the gymnasium, which was in a separate building a block away. We walked in a long line comprised of several cliques along the sidewalk. I marched alone in the procession, playing cards in hand, counting down the minutes until the school day ended.

Then I heard a loud crack. Followed briefly by darkness. I didn't fall, but I staggered. I looked down to see the small rock that had struck me, smaller than a golf ball but large enough to hurt like hell.

The people walking in front of me didn't stop. Neither did the people behind me. A few snickered. The culprit was one of four boys, grouped together, making it difficult to identify the hurler.

I felt a drop of sweat behind my left ear. I wiped it with my hand, then stared at the blood on my fingertips. My attackers giggled as they passed by. They were daring me to retaliate.

I didn't. Instead I retreated to the magic shop. Walt looked at me and determined I needed a couple of stitches, which I never got. When I told Walt what happened, he was shocked that I didn't stand up for myself. "You should've pummeled them!"

Walt had taken me to the boxing gym a few times. He taught me how to take a punch and throw one. He said I hit hard, told me I had "heavy hands." He couldn't understand why I'd walked away from the confrontation. I couldn't either.

I went home with the gash hidden beneath my hair. Mom had enough stress; I didn't see any reason to worry her. But she could tell something was wrong. I downplayed it, saying, "Some kids tried to pick a fight with me today. But I walked away."

"Good for you."

"Is it?" I asked, wanting to understand why I didn't fight back.

Mom explained, "That's not who you are. You've never understood cruelty."

Then she told me a story of which I had no recollection. Apparently, around age four, Mom took me to a park to let me play in a sandbox, where a fight broke out between two boys. I watched in horror as the kids scuffled. Then looked up at my mother to ask, "Why are they doing that?" She didn't remember her response, only my reaction to the violence: I wasn't afraid of it, I was confused by it.

The incident with the rock drove me deeper into my shell. One teacher took notice, Mrs. Rachwitz. A pistol of a woman, she taught history in torn jeans and swore to great effect.

I wrote a paper that made her laugh. She kept me after class to tell me how much she loved it; then we just started talking. She asked about my hobbies. I told her I was interested in sleight-of-hand and illusions.

"I love magic! Do you have a trick for me?"

I politely declined. Getting me to perform was still like pulling teeth. Sometimes I'd visit my mother at the firehouse and she would guilt me into performing for her coworkers, saying, "We spend all day saving lives, the least you could do is show us a card trick!" When that didn't work, she'd back me into a corner, saying, "Do you have any idea how long I was in labor with you?!" At which point, I had no choice but to put on an informal show.

Walt was also confused by my aversion to the spotlight.

"What's the good of learning this stuff if you never show any-one?!" he said, trying to reason with me. Even those closest to me didn't understand: *Concealing my talent* was *the performance*.

"Come on, nothing?" Mrs. Rachwitz said, trying to goad me into showing her "a trick."

I declined again, at which point she moved on.

Our conversations after class grew more frequent and this would become a regular exchange between us. She'd ask me to "do a trick" and I'd reply, "Not today." We both appreciated each other's commitment to the bit.

One day she skipped the banter and said, "I thought of some-thing you should read." She explained that it was an old story about illusions. Had I already known the contents of Plato's *Republic* I wouldn't have rushed to the library to find it.

Mrs. Rachwitz didn't suggest I read the *entire* book, just the one story: the Allegory of the Cave. It took me longer to find that section of the book than it did to read it. I expected some dense philosophical jargon, but it was a simple story about pris-oners, held captive in a cave and forced to watch a show com-posed of shadows.

(SHADOWS)

(PRISONERS)

(WALL)

PLATO'S CAVE

(PUPPETS)

PUPPETEERS

LIGHT

The story resonated with me, but not in the way Mrs. Rachwitz had anticipated. The next day, I stayed after class to dissect it with her.

"What's with the puppeteer?" I asked.

"What do you mean?"

"The story *barely* mentions the puppeteer and then he vanishes. Who was that person? What's with putting shadows on the wall? Was that his job? A hobby? If it *was* his job, why was *that* a job?"

"I'm not sure," she said. "Why do *you* think the puppeteer was there?"

"How should I know?"

I told her I wasn't a philosopher and then accused Plato of being a lazy writer. She tried to move on and discuss other elements of the story—the shadows, the prisoners, and the inexplicable escape. But I couldn't.

For me, the story was centered around a deliberate act of deception. To gloss over that deception, and ignore the motives of the deceiver, was incomprehensible to me. The Universe *wasn't trying* to deceive us when we believed the Earth was at its center. And the Earth *wasn't trying* to pull the wool over our eyes when we believed it was flat. But the puppeteer in the cave *was trying* to deceive those prisoners. And I wanted to know why.

"Well, then we should investigate!" Mrs. Rachwitz said, encouraging me to follow my gut. She suggested I do some more research, but she framed it as a quest. "This story has been around for more than two thousand years, so I'm sure someone has written about the puppeteer. The answer is buried out there somewhere, all we have to do is find it."

I returned to the school library and quickly exhausted its limited resources. Then I sifted through textbooks at the city library, only to leave empty-handed. Internet searches were a bust. After weeks of searching on my own, Mrs. Rachwitz called a philosophy professor at Colorado College, but was given no leads. Even she was surprised by the lack of findings.

What had begun as a noble quest now felt like a chore. Disappointed and defeated, I abandoned our search for the mysterious puppeteer and returned to my shell.

Mrs. Rachwitz tried to find other stories to inspire me, but none of them took. Only now can I see she wasn't trying to educate me. She was trying to bring me back from wherever it was she thought I was going. She saw a quiet kid with potential who was retreating from the world, and she wasn't about to let him go without a fight.

But I was already gone. All I needed was a final push to make it official.

Of all places, it happened in the school library. I was hiding out there, reading a book, when a pencil came sailing across the room, struck me in the chest, and landed in the pages. I looked up to see two brown-haired boys and a girl with straight blond hair seated at the table across from me. All three of them were looking at me. Neither of the boys was from the group that had chucked the rock at my head earlier that semester. I couldn't tell which of them had done it. I pretended not to care; I put the pencil behind my ear and returned to the book.

When the second pencil hit me, Walter's voice played in my head, saying, *Pop the guy who did it and nobody will bother you again.*

"Is there a reason you're throwing pencils at me?" I asked.

The larger of the two boys said, "You got a problem with it?"

I did, in fact, have a problem. And as soon as I figured out which jerk was the culprit, I was going to solve it. I looked down to give them enough time to ready their next projectile. Then I looked up, catching them in the act.

The blond girl was frozen. Her arm was cocked back, holding a pencil. It was her. For a second I thought, *Maybe she's flirting with me.* She relieved me of that fantasy, saying, "What the fuck are you staring at?"

I didn't answer her because I honestly didn't know what I was staring at. Because I didn't know who these people were or why they threw things. Instead of responding, I closed my book, picked up my backpack, and left. I walked out of the library and off school property.

At home, I told my mother I wasn't ever going back. We came to an agreement. I wasn't dropping out of school, I was "taking time off" to "figure things out." On one condition: I must graduate. It didn't matter where or when, I just had to finish. I promised.

It would be more than a year before I sat in another classroom, but eventually we found a way for me to continue my high school education. Typically, I found a loophole in the system: College classes could be applied toward high school credits. That meant I could go to my local community college and walk out of there with a high school diploma. All I had to do was fill out some paperwork and pass the college entry exam. Which I did.

The classes were smaller, filled with students who *chose* to be there. And that choice made all the difference. They were nice people who were trying to better themselves. There were no cliques or social constructs. It was a place to do the work you needed to do so you could get on with the rest of your life.

The flexible schedule allowed me plenty of time to continue my pursuit of arcane knowledge at the magic shop. I even took night classes. I hunkered down, did enough work to make up for the year I'd lost, and graduated on time.

Even after I dropped out of school, I still went back to visit Mrs. Rachwitz. I'd tell her about my progress and she'd tell me about her kids. We talked about the books we had read and the movies we'd seen. Before I left, I'd always show her a trick.

HEAVYWEIGHT

The magic shop opened at 10:00 a.m. Free from the agony of high school, I was usually there at 9:30, sitting in front of the door with cards in hand. Walter would show up holding his morning coffee and I'd ask a question about a technique before he opened the door.

Walt had offered me a job. The catch was that he could only afford to pay me in books: three a week. Considering I had been helping out around the store for months for free, it struck me as a good deal. And while he was technically my boss, the dynamic of our relationship was similar to that of a cantankerous boxing coach and his scrappy young fighter, an analogy I most certainly inherited from Walt.

His grandfather was a Scottish immigrant who made his

drinking money by boxing in bars. The Scotsman trained his son, Walter's dad, to slip jabs and throw mean right hooks, hoping the boy would one day fight for a real title. But Walter's dad was an asthmatic and, instead of going the distance, he ended up repairing refrigerators for a living. That repairman passed his father's dream down to *his* son, Walter.

Walter's world was centered entirely around boxing for the first twenty years of his life. He threw in the towel shortly after he graduated from high school. His father always said he punched like a sissy. The truth was Walter didn't want to hurt his hands; he was protecting them. He wanted to be a magician.

Rather than leaving town to pursue what his father called a "pipe dream," Walter was stuck helping his mother take care of his asthmatic father. Just as Walter didn't fulfill his dad's dream, he also failed to achieve his own goal of becoming one of the great conjurors of the day.

Luckily, the small mountain town where he grew up had a magic shop, in which he started working and ended up owning. He focused on his education, becoming as close to a scholar and theorist as there was in the field of magic. If academic degrees existed in the conjuring arts, Walter most certainly would have had his doctorate.

Neither his son nor his daughter had any interest in magic. Walter wasn't going to force them, he wanted them to choose their own path. I, on the other hand, was desperate to learn from him.

At the shop, I spent the days sorting through new shipments of merchandise and stocking shelves. I shipped orders that were placed by phone. And I demonstrated magic tricks behind the counter, which was the closest I got to performing. Although I didn't see it as such. As I saw it, my job was closer to working at a music store than playing in a band.

Of course, there wasn't a booming scene for magicians in Colorado Springs (or anywhere, for that matter). So, most of the sales had nothing to do with magic: I sold wigs to strippers and cancer patients. I helped elementary schoolteachers obtain the props needed for crude productions of *A Christmas Carol*. I showed kids how to use the blood capsules they bought to scare their parents and offered brutally effective methods for deploying stink bombs.

The shop was located on the main street, so we got our fair share of out-of-towners wandering in. When they left without buying anything, Walter would lecture me, "Why the hell didn't you show them a trick? Don't let them leave without seeing something."

I wasn't keen on selling secrets to tourists. Or anyone for that matter. I was aware of my own hypocrisy in this regard, seeing as I had bought my first book of secrets there. But I found that others didn't appreciate what was offered there. They couldn't see beyond the rubber chickens and top hats. To me, the shop was an informal institution filled with sacred knowledge. To others, we just sold tricks.

Nevertheless, I wanted to keep a roof over Walt's head. I stood behind the counter, right where Walter stood when he first made the knife vanish for me, and I demonstrated the "hot new" products for local aficionados and hooked tourists with "easy-to-master" miracles. Thankfully the good stuff, "the real work" as Walt called it, was buried in books that nobody wanted to read.

When I demonstrated something that involved sleight-of-hand, Walter would watch me out of the corner of his eye. As soon as the customer walked out the door, Walt piped up with his critique.

Once I demonstrated the Cups and Balls* for a customer. When they left without buying anything, Walt didn't even look up from his newspaper to say, "Don't run if you're not being chased."

"What?" I asked.

"You were running."

He was commenting on the manner in which I was sneaking the little red balls under the inverted cups on the table. He meant that I was rushing my movements out of fear of getting caught.

I disputed the charge. "No, I wasn't!"

"Yes, you were."

I had practiced the secret actions (stealing the balls, palming them, loading them under the cups) hundreds of times, maybe thousands, alone in my room. I could do it all in my sleep.

"You weren't even paying attention," I said.

"Yes, I was," he said, still looking at his paper.

"Watch," I said, demanding his attention.

---

* *Cups and Balls*—a classic of conjuring in which small balls appear and disappear under inverted cups.

I executed the actions for him, exactly as I had for the customer, stealing the balls from my pocket, one by one, keeping them palmed, then casually loading them under the cups as I picked them up.

"That's not what you did earlier."

"Yes, it is!"

"Do it for the next customer that comes in."

I practiced at the counter until a lady came in looking for Silly String for her kid's birthday party. After she paid, Walter asked her, "Do you like magic?"

"No," she replied.

"Perfect!" Smiling ear-to-ear.

She agreed to humor me and watched my "little trick."

As I launched into the routine, saying, "As you can see, I have three cups and three little red balls . . . ," Walter stood behind the register with his arms folded, watching me attempt to convert the nonbeliever. Things were going well; I was natural and calm. Then I palmed my first ball.

The moment I stole it from my pocket, I could feel myself hurrying to the first cup on the table. I was even more mindful of my actions on the second cup and, again, I could feel the acceleration. By the third cup I knew Walter was right. And the lady's comment at the conclusion of the routine drove the point home.

When I revealed the balls beneath the cups, she said, "Hey, that was good, I didn't even see you put them there."

Put them there? I wanted her to feel as though the balls had *appeared* under the cups, not as though I had "put them there."

While I never thought she (or anyone) would ever *actually* believe balls materialized out of thin air, that's what I strived for. I wanted to manifest the same sense of wonder that Walter had inspired in me, when he made the knife vanish. The only way to do that, to create that euphoric state of astonishment, was to remove all other possible solutions as to how the event occurred. "You put them there" clearly fell short of that mark.

The lady watching the cups and balls didn't actually see me sneak the balls under the cups. But she intuited that it had happened. My hurried movements caused silent alarms to ring in her head, telling her, *Something's fishy*. It's not that she was particularly perceptive; anyone watching me would have assumed the same.

We've all had someone attempt to hide something from us: The abrupt closing of a laptop when we enter the room. The frantic dash to cover the unwrapped gifts. The sudden body turn after receiving a text message. And just as we've seen others hide something from us, we have felt the surge of fear and adrenaline when we scramble to hide what others aren't meant to see. These are the toxic effects of secrecy.

Secrets enter the system like a drug, causing aberrations in the body and clouds in the mind. The intoxication had caused me to unconsciously hurry when I was sneaking the balls under the cups. But speed is just one of many ways in which a secret can modify our behavior. It can cause us to: Stutter while delivering a plagiarized speech. Avoid eye contact when we see our crush. Or lash out when hiding significant pain.

I summarized both the problem and the solution in a notebook when I wrote: *Secrets are iocane powder. Be the Dread Pirate Roberts.*

After that, I practiced so often I developed a bad habit of blinking every time my hands executed specific moves. It's a common tell* among amateurs, even some professionals. It comes from staring into a mirror for too long. After watching the same action, over and over again, the mind starts to play a clever trick on you. While the *conscious mind* focuses on the actions in the hands, the *subconscious mind* "helps" by having you blink at the exact moment the move occurs.

It's like removing a single frame from a movie. The mind sees the visual hiccup (the ugly moment the move occurs) and cuts it from the narrative. The problem is, while it may appear more deceptive, it only appears that way to *the deceiver.* It's literally a form of self-deception.

When I asked Walt, "How do I fix it?" he replied, "Stop blinking." He was only half-joking, being mindful of it was the first step. But Walt knew I needed a more practical solution.

"Practice without looking at your hands. And instead of using a mirror, use this," he said, loaning me his video camera.

I set the camera on my desk at home and recorded myself practicing. Rather than staring at my hands and focusing on the technique, I allowed my mind to wander, detaching it from the

---

* *Tell*—any unconscious action that divulges information that should otherwise remain hidden.

actions. Then I played back the video, watching myself from outside myself.

Walt said, "Keep the camera for as long as you need. But if you record something great, I get to add it to the collection."

For twenty years, Walter had been archiving magicians' television appearances. Any time a magician performed on a talk show, a variety special, even guest spots on sitcoms and dramas, Walter fired up his VCR and pressed Record. Walter used those tapes as bargaining chips with other collectors across the country, trading his copies for footage he didn't already own. These videos could not be bought or sold, only traded among a small group of very private collectors.

By the time I came around, Walter had amassed a collection of hundreds of tapes, footage of wonder-workers that was otherwise impossible to find. He had clips dating back to 1896 and Georges Méliès's vanishing act, *Escamotage d'une dame chez Robert-Houdin*. A seven-year-old Ricky Jay changing a guinea pig into a dove on the 1955 program *Time for Pets*. Every magician who ever appeared on Johnny Carson's *Tonight Show*. He even had dozens of clips of Carson himself performing magic.

The first clip he ever showed me was arguably the most tragic television appearance of any magician ever: In the 1950s and '60s, Dutch magician Fred Kaps was considered one of, if not *the most*, well-respected conjuror of his generation. The man was a sensational performer, a brilliant technician, an innovator, equally charming on every platform and in multiple languages. After making a name for himself in Europe and the UK, Kaps was ready to take America by storm. His big break came when he was booked on *The Ed Sullivan Show*. The day *after* his impeccable performance, not a single person in America knew who he was or what he did. Because Fred Kaps made his television debut on Sunday, February 9, 1964, following a little band from Liverpool who sang their song "She Loves You."

My favorite videos were the private home recordings of sleight-of-hand legends like: Del Ray. Miller. Grayson. Thompson. These were the guys Walt referred to as "the heavyweights."

We'd order pizza, sit on the couch in the back room, and watch those grainy performances as if they were classic boxing matches. Walter would abruptly stop the tape, saying, *"There! Did you see it? I'll rewind. Watch again."* I saw nothing, which was the point. He'd rewind the tape and replay it over and over, dissecting each movement, the subtle gesture, all the nuances I had missed.

With Walt's guidance, my hands outpaced his within a year and I was able to execute techniques even he couldn't do. He loved it. It became fun for him to see what he could throw at me, giving me harder and harder material, expecting me to throw in the towel. But I never did. I loved seeing the smile on Walt's face when I'd come back the next day performing something he'd failed to learn in his entire life.

Then, one day, I was sitting on a step stool, using a pricing gun to stamp tags onto bottles of disappearing ink, when the phone rang. Walter answered it. After a brief exchange, he transferred the call to the basement, where he could speak in private, which was unusual. Most of the calls we got were people asking if we had whoopee cushions or fake blood. For a guy who owned a magic shop, Walter had surprisingly few secrets.

Thirty minutes later, I heard him coming up the creaky steps. He walked straight up to me and asked, "You own a suit?"

I did not. Walter marched over to the register, removed fifty dollars, and handed it to me. "Go to Goodwill and get something that resembles a suit." I didn't even ask why, I just bolted out the door.

I left the shop wearing jeans and a hoodie and came back wearing a dark brown polyester suit, a white shirt, and the same pair of Converse sneakers. The jacket smelled like cigarettes and the lapels were as wide as my shoulders. The pants fit comfortably, like my baggy blue jeans.

When I returned, Walter was half dressed, wearing black slacks and a white shirt, steaming the wrinkles out of his plaid jacket. He nodded to an old book sitting on the glass countertop.

It was Walter's first-edition copy of *Kartenkünste*, his favorite magic book. He kept it locked in a glass case next to his desk downstairs. "Wrap that up, will ya," he said, tucking his shirt into his unbuckled pants. I grabbed a piece of brown butcher paper and some tape, then wrapped the book as if it were a bomb that could be set off by the slightest movement.

Walter explained what all the fuss was about in a single sentence, saying, "We're going to meet Grayson."

I was finally going to meet a heavyweight. Grayson was widely regarded as one of the greatest sleight-of-hand artists of the modern era. He was the complete package: a brilliant technician and performer, an ingenious inventor of original material, and a historian.

Walt had known Grayson since the '70s, back when Walt was still trying to make it as a performer. They'd found each other working the nightclub circuit and would regularly share "doobies" after their shows. Grayson went on to have the career Walt dreamed of.

Every few years, Grayson would fly in from LA to perform a private show. If he landed within a hundred miles of the Springs, he'd call his old buddy Walt. On this occasion, when the wonderworker came to town to dazzle a group of bankers at the Broadmoor, a five-star hotel seated in the foothills of the Rockies, he called Walt and asked him to meet for drinks after the show. Walt, the mensch that he was, asked Grayson if I could tag along.

If there was an inner circle of magicians, Grayson sat at the head of that table. Walt described him as "old school," because he still believed secrets mattered. And although he was revered by fellow magicians, Grayson had a reputation for being an elitist, as well as being so secretive it bordered paranoia. He wouldn't even touch a deck of cards in the presence of magicians he didn't know and trust. And he certainly didn't know me.

That's why Walt had run downstairs; he was negotiating on my behalf, vouching for me. Somehow, Walt got Grayson to agree to letting me join them. I never asked if the old book I had finished wrapping, one of Walt's prized possessions, was part of that negotiation.

I was ecstatic to meet a conjuring giant. Walt tempered my expectations, making it clear that Grayson wouldn't show me anything. Then he *guaranteed* that I'd have to demonstrate what I was made of. If I wanted to sit at *Grayson's* table, I had to earn it.

Walt laid out the game plan: We'd go and I'd keep my mouth shut. When the time was right, Walter would give me the nod and I'd take out the cards. Walt coached me, saying, "Don't worry about fooling him, that's not the point. Just be yourself and do what you do."

As Walt was grabbing his car keys, the phone rang. It was his wife. I could tell from the look on his face that our meeting was canceled.

Walt hung up and told me the bad news. His wife had slipped and thought she might have broken her tailbone. He had to go. But then he surprised me with: "His show finishes in an hour. You need to get to the Broadmoor. He'll meet you in the study with the three couches."

He wanted me to go meet Grayson alone. I told him I couldn't do it. He told me I had to, handing me the neatly wrapped book. Then he rushed to his wife's rescue. I threw the book in my backpack and set out to the Broadmoor.

It was three miles from the magic shop. I wasn't old enough to drive, and it had snowed the night before, so I rode my bike through freezing slush. I raced the sun as it set behind the tallest mountain in the state, Pike's Peak. Cars splashed muck on me as they passed. By the time I arrived, my face was numb and my new suit drenched. I didn't care; I was about to meet a hero.

I entered the hotel lobby like a wet mutt. I had never seen anything like this place. A lavish chandelier shimmered in the center of a ceiling made entirely of stained glass. The walls were a dark oak, with old paintings you'd expect to find at a museum. Being careful not to slip on the white marble floor, I made my way inside.

A concierge snidely asked, "Excuse me, can I help you?"

"I'm looking for my father," I said, brushing him off with a lie as I continued my quest.

I found the study with three couches. It was a cozy den with high ceilings. The bookshelves were the same dark wood, stocked floor to ceiling with literary classics. Three leather sofas squared off in front of a grand fireplace. I plopped down on one of the couches and warmed up by the crackling fire.

An hour passed and still no sign of Grayson. Normally, I would have passed the time by fiddling with a deck of cards. But I wanted to make a good first impression. Going by his reputation, I thought he might just walk the other way if he saw me with cards in my hand. Better safe than sorry; I kept the cards in their case.

After two hours I was bored and fidgety, so I took out the cards. Then I heard a deep voice say, "You must be Walter's friend."

He looked so much older than the man I'd seen performing on Walt's VHS tapes. Most of his dark hair had turned gray; his face was gruff and parts of it drooped. He wore a black three-piece suit, but his coat was draped over his shoulders like a cape. On his head was a fedora and he was holding a drink, a reward for what I could only imagine had been a magnificent show.

I scrambled to put the cards out of sight, shoving them under a couch pillow. I stood up to shake his hand. Then I reached into my backpack to retrieve his gift.

He grumbled, "Thanks," setting the book aside as his eyes clocked the cards I had tried to hide. He muttered, "You do anything with those?"

I stammered, "Um. Yes. I mean, I think so."

"Let's see it."

This was it, the opportunity I had been waiting for. All I had to do was show him one of the knuckle-busting miracles I had been working on. He'd see my potential and immediately teach me everything he knew.

Grayson removed his hat and placed his coat on the back of a chair before sitting across from me. Using the glass coffee table between us as the stage for my hands, I proceeded to perform an incredibly complex (and in hindsight, extremely boring) card trick.

I looked up to see his reaction. There was none. I desperately wanted him to say something, until he did.

"That it?" he asked.

"No, no," I said, assuring him the best was yet to come.

I tried to earn his favor again, this time by performing a variation on the old "pick a card, any card" theme. And, again, he was underwhelmed. As he picked up his hat I could feel my future slipping away. I blurted out, "Oh, and there's this one thing . . ."

I didn't even know how that sentence was going to end. I just needed to buy time. He sat there as I searched through the cards, racking my brain for something, *anything* that would impress him. But I drew a complete blank.

Out of desperation, I decided not to perform a trick. Instead

I would demonstrate a muck* that I had learned from an old manuscript I'd found on Walt's bookshelf. No story, no razzle-dazzle, purely a demonstration of skill. It was a Hail Mary.

I handed him the deck of cards, told him to shuffle, and said, "Deal me two cards."

As Grayson shuffled, I remember wondering if he noticed that I had stolen two Kings from the deck before I handed it to him. He dealt me two cards.

"Fair?" I asked.

After he nodded, I immediately picked up the two cards and, in the action of turning them faceup, I switched them for the Kings I had kept hidden in the palm of my hand.

I'll never forget his reaction. Grayson looked up at me, smiled, and said, "That's a hell of a move."

He asked me to do it again. So I did. Then, to my utter surprise, Grayson reached into his pocket and removed a deck of cards. I spent the next three hours learning at the feet of a master.

The next day at the magic shop I told Walter about my triumphant encounter. I told him about the move I demonstrated and how much Grayson liked it. Marveling at how a single move got Grayson to open up to me, I asked Walt, "Why do you think that impressed him so much?"

He replied, "Because he's never met anyone who can do it."

———

* *Muck*—a switch of cards in a game. A *mucker* or *hand mucker* is a cheater who specializes in switching cards. (Note: In poker, the discards are referred to as "the muck.")

The following day, Walt showed up holding his coffee in one hand and a paper sack in the other, which he tucked behind the counter. When I asked, "What's in the bag?" he replied, "None of your damn business." I knew it was something good.

At the end of that long and particularly tiring day, as I was turning the lights off around the store, Walt said, "Don't forget to take this," holding the paper sack he had tucked away when he first arrived. As he handed it to me, he said, "I'll want these back."

He had loaned me plenty of things before, but they never came with such a firm condition. I peeked into the bag at a four-volume set of VHS tapes I had never heard of: *Steve Forte's Gambling Protection Series*.

Mr. Forte wasn't a magician. He was a game protection spe-cialist who worked with the casino industry, helping with theft prevention. And his video series had nothing to do with magic; they were educational tapes from the 1980s, produced to help educate people on the techniques used by gambling cheats.

I looked at Walt, confused by what I had just been handed.

He said, "You nail this stuff and you can do anything."

THE REAL DEAL

The conversation went something like this:

"Mom, I need to borrow your car."

"Why?"

"I need to go to Denver."

"Why do you need to go to Denver?"

"There's a guy I have to meet."

"What guy?"

"A card guy, someone Walt said I should meet."

"When?"

"Tomorrow."

"No, I have errands to run."

"But I gotta go! He's only in town one day."

"Then I guess you better take the bus."

"Fine . . . But you're okay with me going?"

"When will you be home?"

"Late."

"How late?"

"Not sure. But late."

"Who did you say you're meeting?"

"A card guy Walt said I should meet. This is my one chance."

Other parents probably would not have allowed their teenage son to make that unaccompanied eighty-mile trip on a Greyhound bus to meet a stranger. Thankfully, other parents weren't my mother. Years later, I asked her why she granted me the freedom to pursue my interests. She replied, "You never gave me a reason to not trust you."

I tended to agree with her. Oddly enough, the reasons I had given for dropping out of high school were the *same reasons* my mother trusted me. I shared no interests with my peers: I didn't enjoy attending or throwing parties; I never drank or smoked; I wasn't obsessed with video games or even television. As a teenager I was, in a word, boring.

Of course, *I* didn't think I was boring. My days were spent working in a store surrounded by arcane knowledge and rubber chickens. There I had interesting conversations with curious characters of every shade and stripe. When I wasn't at the shop, I was practicing sleight-of-hand. And the best place to do that was at home, because that's where all my books were.

For a moment, my mother feared that I wasn't socializing enough with others my own age; she worried I was missing out on the teenage experience. Then she remembered *her* teenage experience.

As a firefighter in a town ravaged by meth and riddled with runaways, she had seen the absolute worst of my generation. With so little to do in town, it was easy to find trouble. By comparison, she realized I was doing pretty damn well: I had Walt, the great mentor who helped me keep my eyes on the prize, and Maggie, his kind wife, who made sure I was taking care of myself. I had made friends with customers and the additional help Walt hired in the holiday season. They were nice, intelligent people, mostly twenty-year-olds, trying to figure out life. Just like me. Just like my mom.

My mother and I *genuinely* enjoyed each other's company, partly because we had, in a sense, grown up together, but also because *we were still growing up together*. When I was seventeen years old, my mother was only thirty-four. And she was, by any measure, "cooler" than me; she introduced me to Nirvana and Prince, took me to see *Pulp Fiction;* in the winter we'd go snowboarding together, in the summer we'd go rock climbing, both her ideas. She also pulled grown men out of burning buildings for a living.

And I really was *always* honest with her. The one time I pocketed her five bucks, I fessed up minutes later. I called her immediately after I had accidentally shot bottle rockets through her Gay Pride flag in the backyard, when I could have easily disposed of the evidence and played the iggy.* And there was the

---

* *Play the iggy*—gambling slang for feigning ignorance or playing dumb.

day after I lost my virginity, a personal milestone I might not have shared with Mom had I not been rattled by having just driven my girlfriend to the pharmacy to buy a Plan B pill.

I didn't lie to my mother for one simple reason: She had never given me a reason to lie to her.

But . . .

When I told her that I wanted to go to Denver to meet "a card guy," that was true. I had been searching for him for months. But I might not have told her the *whole* truth. I didn't tell her what kind of card guy he was.

He was a card cheat.

The hunt began not long after Walt loaned me the Steve Forte videos on "casino game protection." The night he gave me those tapes, I went home and pressed Play on volume one. It opened with cheesy lounge music and a green title card with a corny font that only existed in the '80s. The production value was equivalent to a corporate video from HR.

Most of the footage consisted of the same scene shot from various angles: Mr. Forte, a clean-cut fellow in a gray blazer, seated at a green-felt card table, shot from the neck down to focus attention on his hands, which held a deck of blue border-less cards.

Forte began to narrate: *"Welcome to our four-part gambling protection series. Hi, my name is Steve Forte and here's a few interesting facts before we begin: Did you know that people of all ages gamble with cards more than any other hobby, pastime, or participant sport? Accord-*

ing to the United States Playing Card company, last year approximately 120 million decks of cards were sold in this country. No doubt, card playing is one of the favorite sources of entertainment . . ."

Just as Forte was beginning to lull me to sleep with his gentle Bostonian accent, he began to casually shuffle the cards on the table, as if he were a dealer in a casino. After a few mixes, he gave the deck what appeared to be a fair cut, then casually revealed the four aces that were on top.

I leaned toward the screen as Forte shuffled again, continuing, *"The fact is, millions of dollars have changed hands in games played with cards. A sad truth, though, is that most of these games, with very few exceptions, would be exposed to and victimized by some form of cheating at one time or another . . ."*

Forte finished another series of shuffles and cuts (which I would have sworn were real), then dealt out five poker hands. When he showed the four aces in *his* hand, I didn't understand what I was witnessing. I knew how to control cards, but not like this.

"That's what this video series is all about. In these tapes I will demonstrate and expose numerous card cheating techniques. There will be tips on detecting these moves in games. And procedures to help you prevent both the amateur and professional cheater from playing in your game. So let's get started with volume one: Cheating at Cards."

That night I made it through three of the four videos. I dreamed of all the things I had never seen before: riffle stacking,[*]

---

[*] *Riffle stacking*—to secretly arrange cards in the action of shuffling.

peeks,* and coolers.† Then I woke up early and watched volume four.

What I found even more astonishing than the barrage of techniques I had never seen before was Forte's execution of the moves I *was* familiar with. I had seen plenty of other magicians perform false deals‡ and false shuffles.§ And I could spot the moves a mile away. The little glitches and hiccups that went unnoticed by laymen were glaringly obvious to anyone who studied like I had. But watching Forte, I felt as though I was seeing them for the first time. In his hands, the secret actions were seamlessly (*perfectly!*) integrated with the natural actions. False shuffles looked like *real* shuffles. False deals looked like *real* deals. There were times I thought he must have been faking the demonstration. But then, sure enough, he'd show the move again from another angle, or in slow motion, to reveal he was really doing what he claimed to be doing. Every lie he performed with his hands looked so confident, so effortless. So . . . honest.

I went into the shop and asked Walt, "How is he so good?"

"He's the real deal."

---

* *Peek*—to secretly glimpse the identity of a card.

† *Cooler*—a prearranged deck that is secretly switched into play. The name comes from the fact that the temperature of the deck that is being switched in is slightly cooler than the deck that has been in use on the table.

‡ *False deal*—to simulate the action of dealing cards off the top of the deck while secretly dealing them from other positions.

§ *False shuffle*—to simulate the action of shuffling cards, maintaining their order.

Walt told me the rumor that before Forte was protecting casinos, he was beating them. He didn't learn sleight-of-hand to entertain and amuse; he learned it to cheat. Which meant he couldn't afford to make any mistakes. The slightest slip of a card could have led to severe repercussions. Forte's superlative technique reflected those high stakes.

I spent six months locked in my room with the Forte tapes. I practiced so much, I went through two to three decks a day. When I finally felt like I had taken the techniques as far as I could on my own, I went to Walt for pointers. But when I asked him for tips on how to improve, something strange occurred.

Rather than picking my technique apart and offering suggestions on how to improve, he just shrugged and said, "Looks good to me."

That surprised me because even I could see the flaws. We had a similar exchange again later that week, after I showed him a muck I had learned from the tapes. The third time it happened, after I asked him for tips on the tabled faro,* I knew something was up.

"Are you mad at me?" I asked Walt.

"No, not at all." He sounded sincere.

"Are you sure?"

"Yeah, why? Are you okay?"

I told him I was fine and clarified why I was asking him. Walt explained he wasn't being passive-aggressive or dodging my

---

* *Tabled faro*—a shuffle that involves splitting the deck into equal halves, then perfectly interlacing the cards.

questions. He wanted to help; he just didn't know how. For the first time in the five years we'd known each other, he didn't have answers I was looking for.

I had known that magicians and card cheats were different breeds of deceiver. But I thought, at the very least, there was an intersection where they exchanged tools (false shuffles, false deals, palming, switches, shifts, controls, etc.). I was wrong. It was not an intersection. It was a one-way street. And the direction that road traveled surprised me.

Virtually all of the techniques that magicians and cheaters "share" come from the world of the cheater. For hundreds, possibly thousands of years, magicians have taken tools from cheaters and offered little in return. Or, more likely, cheaters didn't want what magicians had to offer. It's not that the magician's methods are inferior. It's that they have an entirely different relationship to deception.

Magicians broadcast their deception. They take credit for their illusions by pointing to their secrets. They don't reveal their privileged information, but they admit to having it, flaunting it with flourishes and winks. Magicians are theatrical. And they use that theatricality to help perpetrate the deception. Is he waving his hands like that for dramatic effect, or does he need to move in that manner to execute the secret action? Is he wearing those out-of-date coattails to look dapper, or to hide the doves? Is he telling us this to fill time and "entertain" us, or does he need to say this to justify the actions necessary for the effect? Magicians are not obligated to adhere to the rituals and behaviors of the natural world. Because they exist in the realm of fantasy, their work is fiction. They are performers, and they do not hide the fact that they are performing. Other than ridicule, there are no negative consequences for seeming unnatural.

For cheaters, the stakes are too high. They are not afforded the luxuries of attention, unnaturalness, and flair; the cheater seeks to remain invisible. Must remain invisible. Which means their actions and behavior, the clothes they wear, the way they speak—it must all appear natural. Their illusions must always be seen as truths.

So, when I asked Walt for help, he was at a loss. Gambling sleights were out of his wheelhouse and he wasn't one to posture. He knew I wanted *real* answers and that any tips he might offer would be contrary to my goals.

I asked Walt if he knew Steve Forte. When he said he didn't, I asked him if he knew any cheaters. "I've met one or two over the years, but I wouldn't say I know any," Walt said, adding, "I'll ask around."

There were a few challenges trying to locate a professional card cheat. One was geography. I was unlikely to find any cheats in my little mountain town, or even catch them passing through.

Another problem was scarcity. At the turn of the twenty-first century, there were *very few* professional card mechanics still living in the wild. Sure, there were amateurs who dealt from the bottom in friendly games. But the *professionals* were no longer using sleight-of-hand. Just like the rest of the world, crooked gamblers had gone digital.

The gritty, streetwise mechanics were being replaced by egg-heads from MIT. Card mechanics were relics of a soon-to-be-forgotten era, and their techniques were considered barbaric compared to the sophisticated computers used to gain an edge at the gaming tables. The tech could make you more money in half the time at the table and save you god knows how many hours of practice. Why spend thousands of hours learning how to control a single playing card when you can know the position of every card in the deck with the push of a single button?

Finally, there was the simple fact that cheaters don't want to be found. They don't write books or give lectures on their work. They don't seek applause or accolades. To do so would jeopardize their secret practice. While I respected their commitment, it was frustrating as hell. Like the gunslingers of the Wild West, it seemed that card mechanics had left our world and entered the realm of North American folklore.

Then Walt got the call. A friend of a friend connected him to the cheat Walt had crossed paths with fifteen years earlier. His name was Ronnie and he was going to be in Denver in a week. He was only staying in town for two days.

Based on their mutual acquaintance's respect for Walt, Ronnie had agreed to sit down with me. All I had to do was get to Denver. After failing to borrow Mom's car, the following day I purchased a bus ticket.

I was surprised to see the tickets were so cheap, but the moment I got on the bus, I understood why. Filthy floors. Stained seats. I sat near the front, hoping one of three pine tree–shaped air fresheners hanging from the driver's mirror would help mask the scent of sweat.

I arrived at the Greyhound station in Denver, praying I didn't smell like the bus. I had to take a short cab ride to Five Points, a neighborhood not far from the baseball stadium, Coors Field. The meeting was scheduled for 7:00 p.m. I arrived at 4:00 and wandered around the neighborhood until I found a mom-and-pop Mexican restaurant, where I ate tacos, drank Cherry Coke, and fiddled with cards.

Unable to contain my excitement, I headed to the meeting place fifteen minutes early. A sun-faded blue sign that said BILLIARDS hung above a dingy red awning. The sun was still out, but inside the bar it was already dark as night. It reeked of cigarettes, but I preferred it to the bus. Loud music played over a sea of chattering and the clacking of balls.

I got about three feet past the door before the bartender stopped me and asked for ID. (Walt didn't mention anything about an age restriction, because it never occurred to him to ask.)

I gave the bartender my ID as if admittance were determined by moxie and not age.

"You can't be here, man," the bartender said, handing me back my ID.

"I'm looking for my dad," I said.

The bartender chuckled and said, "You think your father is here?"

"Yes," I replied, unsure of the joke.

Humoring me, he said, "All right. Do a lap, but then you gotta go."

I waded through the room. Players hunched over pool tables spilled into the center aisle. I was careful to avoid their back-swings as they took their shots. As I moved deeper into the hall, it dawned on me why the bartender had chuckled when I told him I was looking for my father: I was the only white person in the building.

I scanned the room. I had been told that Ronnie was in his mid-forties. He was about my height, possibly a little shorter, thin, but not that athletic-looking. I would have needed to shout Ronnie's name to cull him from the crowd, had it not been for the only useful bit of information that Walt gave me. He described the hat Ronnie "always" wore. "It's black. A cross between a baseball cap and a beret."

He was describing what I would later realize was a Kangol hat. And the reason Walt remembered this hat fifteen years after meeting Ronnie that one single time was because it wasn't just a hat; it was also a holdout.[*]

In card games, as Ronnie sat down at the card table, he would take his hat off and set it in his lap, interior side up. Inside the hat was a secret pocket that concealed the deck that would be switched in. After secretly exchanging one deck for another, Ronnie would drop the straight deck into the hat, then discreetly push it into the secret pocket. Even if someone got suspicious and looked in his hat, it appeared to be "clean."

---

[*] *Holdout*—a term for any number of secret devices used to conceal one or more cards in a game. The idea being: You can't just sit there with cards in your lap, and you certainly can't hide them in your palm all night. It's even too risky to have them loose in a pocket. They need to be hidden, secure, and readily available. The holdout acts as a card caddy, patiently (and discreetly) holding your cards until the time has come to conceal, retrieve, and/or switch cards.

There were two guys wearing that same hat at the pool hall: One was wearing a white shirt you'd expect to see in Cuba during the summer. The other was wearing a Dallas Cowboys' jersey, number twenty-two.

I had narrowed it down, but both guys fit the loose description I had of Ronnie. So I did the only thing I could think of. I pulled out my deck of cards and fiddled with them as I passed by the likely candidates. Both guys noticed me. But only one of them stared at my hands.

I approached the man in the Cubano shirt and said, "Excuse me, are you Ronnie?"

Slightly perplexed by the appearance of the teenage boy in front of him, he removed the toothpick he was chewing on to reply, "Last I checked." His southern accent instantly softened his image.

"I'm Walter's friend."

"Oh right. He here, too?"

Just then, the bartender started to make his way over. My time was up.

I said, "No, he's not, it's just me," quickly adding, "But I was hoping you'd have some time to sit down?"

"All right, kid, let's go," the bartender said.

"One second," I said, waiting to hear Ronnie's answer.

The bartender looked at Ronnie and, nodding my way, said, "You know this kid?"

Ronnie looked at me for a moment, then back at the bartender to say, "Yeah, he's cool."

The bartender turned around and walked the other way.

"You're a magician, too?" he asked.

I wasn't sure how to answer. Or if there was a right answer. But before I could offer any answer, Ronnie said, "Let's see a trick."

Feeling ambushed, I said, "Oh, um . . . Sure."

The pressure mounted as Ronnie waved over his friends and an entourage of men holding cue sticks gathered around me. I was ready to demonstrate moves for Ronnie, one-on-one, not put on an impromptu show for his friends. With the pool table behind me and a half dozen men in front, I was trapped.

I racked my brain for ideas. The few that came to me were bad. I spread the cards, looking at their faces, hoping one would trigger an idea. Nothing. Then I noticed the man standing to my left was holding a beer bottle.

I extended the cards to that man and said, "Here, take these." The moment he took the cards with his free hand, I said, "Give them a shuffle," and then I held my other hand out, knowing he'd need to hand me the beer in order to shuffle.

As he clumsily mixed the cards, I casually placed his bottle on the edge of the pool table by my side. I took the pack of cards back, had him select a card, told him to remember it, then lost the card back into the deck. With a few well-choreographed actions, I caused the card to seemingly vanish from the deck and "materialize" inside the beer bottle on the table.

It took a moment for anyone to notice the card bobbing in the beer. Then one guy broke the silence with "What the fuck?" and the rest of the crowd started to catch on, creating a swelling chorus of "No way" and "Hell no." Everyone went wild except Ronnie. He gave nothing away.

The crowd dispersed, returning to their pool tables, leaving Ronnie and me to conduct our business. Ronnie asked a polite version of the question "So who are you and what do you want?"

I told him I was a fan of his work, despite having never seen it. And that I just wanted to meet him and, perhaps, get some pointers.

We sat at a table in the back for the next couple of hours. Some of that time was spent with me shuffling and him watching, correcting my form along the way. Ronnie barely touched the cards, only taking them from me occasionally to show me what I was doing wrong, then handing them right back. The little I saw was enough for me to see he was special. But, to my surprise, most of the advice he gave me that day had nothing to do with my technique.

"You got the hands, kid. You should start focusing on the story."

"What do you mean? Like patter?"

"Nah, it's deeper than that. It can't feel rehearsed, like a script. It's gotta feel real. You gotta get it in your bones."

"How do I do that?"

"There's no easy answer, man. Like Miles said, 'It takes a long time to sound like yourself.'"

I assumed Miles was one of his friends. Straining to understand, I asked him for an example of what he was talking about. Referring to the card trick I had performed for his friends earlier, he said, "You were telling them what *you* wanted them to hear. You need to let them *tell themselves* the story."

I asked him if there was a book I could read on this subject.

He chuckled. "You ain't gonna find it in a book, man." But then, perhaps sensing I was struggling to grasp the concept, he threw me a bone, saying, "You heard of Titanic Thompson?"

I had not.

"Check him out. That guy got it."

He was born Alvin Thomas in 1893, in a small Missouri town. Somehow this dirt-poor, uneducated (illiterate, in fact!) kid from the Ozarks went on to make millions and go down in history as arguably the greatest hustler of all time, Titanic Thompson.

Titanic, or "Ti" as his friends called him, made his first mark as a pool shark, traveling from town to town, wandering into billiard halls and beating every guy in the joint. After he slayed the room, he'd ask, "Who's the best cue in the state?" Then Ti would track that player down and beat him, too.

It was rumored he got his nickname after surviving the sinking of the unsinkable *Titanic*, in 1912. People said that he had conned his way onto a life raft by dressing like a woman and cradling a sack of potatoes like a baby.

But that wasn't true.

Two weeks after the *Titanic* sank, dragging more than 1,500 souls down with it, a long-limbed teenager wearing a raggedy brown suit moseyed into Snow Clark's pool hall in Joplin, Missouri. After beating every player there—including the owner, Mr. Snow Clark himself—the lanky lad noticed a sign in the window that read: $200 TO ANY MAN WHO JUMPS OVER MY NEW POOL TABLE.

The sign was clearly rhetorical, a humorous attempt to lure tourists inside. The table in question was nine feet long and as high as your hip. You'd have to be an Olympic athlete to clear it. And even if you did clear it, you'd break a leg or bust your skull landing on the other side.

The young man looked at the table, then turned around and said, "I'll take that bet."

Mr. Clark and the rest of the room laughed at him, called him a fool. The young man stormed out. Ten minutes later he returned, dragging behind him the mattress he'd just purchased at the motel across the street. He placed the mattress at one end of the table, then walked around to the other side. After giving himself a running start, the kid leaped headfirst over the table, flipping and landing comfortably on his back on the mattress.

As Clark watched the kid collect his winnings, someone asked, "What's his name?" Clark replied, "No idea. But it ought to be Titanic 'cause he just sank us all."

After that, Ti went on to hustle golf pros. His secret? He was better at golfing than they were. That, and he trained himself to be ambidextrous. After setting the suckers up, playing with his right hand, he'd switch to his natural, more dominant left hand and show them what he could really do. Anyone who played him said he could have dominated the professional circuit. But Ti had no interest in fair play. Where's the fun in that?

Ti expanded his repertoire, cheating at cards and scamming

dice games. Rigging horseshoe tosses and checkers matches. He even carried a two-headed quarter around for coin tosses. He actually had the stones to hand his opponent the crooked quarter and call heads. If the mark noticed the coin was gaffed, Ti would play it off as a joke. If they didn't, he'd take the money.

But what he really became notorious for were his proposition bets. These were the little side bets that had nothing to do with whatever game he was actually playing.

He'd pick up a walnut that had fallen from a tree and say, "I bet you I can throw this over that building." Anyone who'd ever touched a walnut knew that was impossible. Walnuts are too light, easily swayed by the wind. Ti would be lucky to get it across the street, let alone over the tall building. Once the bet was agreed to, Ti would launch the walnut into the sky and clear the building with ease.

Little did the sucker know, Ti always carried around a walnut that he'd filled with lead, which he'd secretly drop on the ground before "finding" it. He later used peanuts when they became popular and more readily available. He once tried the infamous ruse on Al Capone.

The story goes: Ti played cards with Capone. After the game, outside, Ti claimed to have a better arm than any Major League Baseball pitcher. Capone called bullshit and told him to prove it. As luck would have it, there was a fruit stand right there. Ti bought a lemon (which he had loaded with buckshot and placed there earlier that evening), looked at the five-story building across the street, and said, "I bet you five hundred bucks I can get this onto that roof."

Capone looked up at the building and said, "I'll take that bet." But as Ti cocked his arm back, Capone said, "Wait." Capone then bought a lemon of his own, which he placed onto the ground and proceeded to step on, crushing it. He picked up the sticky mess and handed it to Ti, saying, "Throw this one."

Ti had no choice but to throw what the gangster handed him. Capone then watched as Ti took a few skips and hurled the mangled fruit into the air, across the street, and onto the roof, barely clearing the ledge. Capone smiled and said, "You really are a versatile son of a bitch."

But it was the "twenty miles to Joplin" story that helped me understand what Ronnie meant by "let them *tell themselves* the story."

Ti took a regular fishing trip with two buddies. On one particular trip, driving to the fishing hole, the three men saw a work crew on the opposite side of the roadway, installing a sign that read: 20 MILES TO JOPLIN.

The next day, they saw the sign again on their way back into town. Ti scoffed and said, "That sign is in the wrong spot. It's not twenty miles from here. More like fifteen miles."

The two friends disagreed with Ti: "They measure it out, there's no way it's that far off."

"I'll bet you a hundred we are less than fifteen miles from town," Ti said.

"Let's make it five hundred," one of his pals said.

"Boys, you got a bet."

The trio drove back to town in silence with their eyes glued to the odometer. Wouldn't you know it, the trip was just under fifteen miles. What Ti didn't tell them: After passing the sign the first time, he had gone back that night and moved it five miles down the road.

It wouldn't have worked had the three men not witnessed the road crew installing the sign. Ti knew his friends saw what he saw. And he knew that the three men would be passing that sign again on their way back, which meant he also knew the story they were going to tell themselves *later*. He knew that when they passed the sign again, they'd remember the workers who installed it. So, as if to travel into the future, Ti got ahead of them in that story and altered it without their knowing. When it came time to swindle his pals, all Ti needed to do was state the truth, knowing they'd sell themselves on the lie.

Ronnie went back to his home in Vegas. It'd be a year before I'd see him again. But he gave me his number so we could stay in touch. The first time I called him was to tell him I'd read all about Titanic Thompson. I asked him if he'd ever met Ti, which he had not. But he casually stated that he owned a lead-filled walnut, once carried—but never thrown—by Titanic Thompson himself.

I waited a few weeks before calling him again, to ask him for advice about a maneuver that was giving me trouble. I used my shoulder to hold the phone against my ear, freeing my hands up to handle the cards, so I could follow along. This became a regular ritual.

I'd practice for a week or two, then call Ronnie again to let him know my progress and to ask about a new technique. He never answered his phone. Instead, he let it go to voicemail and only called back if I left a message. He never took more than a day to get back to me. My phone would ring and I'd know it was him because the caller ID said: UNKNOWN CALLER.

Ronnie was generous with his time; some calls lasted several hours. I appreciated our conversations, but after a few months I began to feel guilty that I didn't have anything to offer him; our relationship had become a one-way street.

But then, about six months after we first met, he called me, asking me about a move I had described to him. He didn't know about it and, at the time, didn't seem interested. But he was, and after we hung up, he looked into it so he could learn it. When he couldn't find it—because he didn't remember the name correctly—he called me to get the info again, which I eagerly gave him. I was thrilled to have something, anything, to offer him.

After that, instead of automatically letting me go to voicemail, Ronnie answered the phone whenever I called. And he continued to call me, unprompted. He'd ask me what I was working on or if I had anything new to share. Sometimes he just wanted to chat.

Once he said he hadn't been feeling well, he'd been suffering from nausea and various aches and pains. He thought it was the flu, but it wasn't the season and he said it had been going on for more than a week. I urged him to visit a doctor, but he wasn't the type. He sounded like he was in pain, so I put him on the phone with my mother to see if she could help diagnose the problem.

She asked him a series of questions, employing her best bed-side manner. I leaned in to listen as he answered, "Yes, ma'am," "No, ma'am," always calling her "ma'am," despite being a decade older than she was. The next day, Ronnie called me from a hospital bed, sounding more like himself. He said, "Your mom was right, it was kidney stones." Then he asked for our address. A few days later, a box arrived, addressed to my mother. Inside were six or seven peaches, a bag of flour, sugar, various other spices, and Ronnie's most cherished secret: his mother's recipe for peach cobbler.

One year after we first met, Ronnie called to tell me he'd be passing through Denver again, in two weeks' time. He took an annual road trip to his hometown, Knoxville. He refused to fly anywhere, so he drove from Las Vegas. Along the way, he stopped in towns where he could see familiar faces. Denver was one of those stops, and I was now a familiar face.

"Who's going with you?" I asked about his trip to Tennessee.

When he said, "No one," I blurted out, "Want some company?"

ROAD TRIP

The plan: Ronnie would pick me up, we'd spend a week making our way to Tennessee, and I'd fly home from there.

I asked Ronnie if he was playing in any card games along the way. He assured me he was not, saying, "If I was, you wouldn't be coming."

My mother didn't object to me going. I was eighteen, and soon I wouldn't even be living under her roof. Nevertheless, Ronnie assured her he'd get me home safely. We took turns driving his maroon Honda Accord, switching seats when we stopped for gas. At one of those gas stations, we both saw a man get into his car without noticing he had just dropped his wallet on the sidewalk. Ronnie ran over, picked up the wallet, then tapped on the guy's window to give it back to him. It was a perfect example of what made him such a fascinating character. He was simultaneously the most honest man I knew and the most artful deceiver I had ever met. After a hundred miles on the road together, I felt comfortable enough to ask him the obvious question: "How the hell did *you* end up cheating at cards for a living?" It took the rest of the trip to get the answer.

Ronnie grew up in Knoxville. Like me, he never knew his father. Unlike me, he had siblings: two brothers—one older, one younger—and a much younger sister. He wanted to be a musician when he was a kid, a dream he picked up when he found the trumpet his older brother had abandoned. He joined the band at school.

His aspirations of becoming a jazz musician ended on his fourteenth birthday, when his older brother told him it was time to start earning his keep. Ronnie was given a choice: learn how to deal drugs or deal cards. He chose the latter and began practicing sleight-of-hand.

I was surprised to learn Ronnie had an interest in magic. At some point, he got his hands on a book considered at that time to be the bible of card cheating, *The Expert at the Card Table*. Written and published pseudonymously in 1902, it contained a large section on card cheating techniques followed by an equally large one on card tricks of the era. He was fascinated by both aspects of card handling, and by the time he graduated from high school he'd read the book multiple times and could quote the text from memory.

He started out assisting his brother in back-alley craps games, turning players' heads, distracting them to provide cover for his brother, who'd switch the dice. When he was sixteen, he joined his brother at the card table. He began honing his skills: bottom dealing, reading marked cards, holding out good cards and switching them in to make better hands for himself or his partner.

He worked on ringing in* "coolers" that gave one player a good hand and another player, usually Ronnie's brother, an even better hand. The sleight-of-hand challenges involved in switching an entire deck of cards without anyone noticing are significant, but, as Ronnie told it, the results were worth it.

At nineteen he joined the navy to get away from what he described as "a rough neighborhood." He was stationed in San Francisco and had access to a magic shop. He spent his time feeding his interest in magic during days off and playing poker with other sailors at night, for pocket money. They never stood a chance against him. Although the money wasn't huge, the regular opportunity to continue honing his skills turned out to be invaluable. Ronnie thought he was going to spend the rest of his life in the navy. But life had other plans for him.

A few weeks before Ronnie's twenty-first birthday, his older brother was killed in a car accident. Ronnie returned home for the funeral and never went back to the ship. Instead he stayed behind to help his family, filling the emotional and financial void his brother's death left behind.

---

* *Ring in*—to secretly switch a card into play.

As we drove across the eastern border of Colorado into Kansas, Ronnie told me how he'd ended up in Las Vegas.

Not long after he returned home, on the advice of a friend, Ronnie packed up his car and drove to Sin City. He was told he could get a job dealing poker in one of the major hotels. This was the late 1970s, and the Mob still ran the town in those days. Believe it or not, not all the poker games were on the up-and-up, even on the Strip.

Ronnie went to the Stardust and inquired about becoming a dealer. They were interested. His audition was fairly straightforward: He had to demonstrate his ability to false shuffle and false cut a deck of cards, execute a second deal,* and stack the deck. Not an easy test; there were few people who could do even one of those techniques, let alone all of them.

Ronnie auditioned at a poker table in a back office. He shuffled and dealt dozens of times under the watchful eyes of three somber men, each wearing a white shirt and black slacks. They never said a word, but at some point one of them nodded his approval to the poker room manager, who stood watching from the door.

The three silent observers turned out to be card mechanics already on the payroll at the Stardust. Although Ronnie was young, he was clearly talented and was hired on the spot. His job was to deal fairly—most of the time. But on occasion, when needed, he had to kick in a cooler for the casino's Mob owners.

---

* *Second deal*—to deal the second card from the top of the deck.

Most of the regular poker players were allowed to play unmolested. The cold-deck* strategy was used primarily to get money back from any outsider who had recently won big at the craps or blackjack tables. Having the poker room manager bring over the pre-stacked decks every hour or so during regularly scheduled deck changes eliminated any need to switch the cards via sleight-of-hand. It's a timeworn but still extremely effective way to cheat.

Dealing poker for the Mob, Ronnie found himself making between $3,000 and $5,000 a week, $150,000 to $250,000 a year, a hell of a lot of money in late 1970s dollars. There was just one problem. He'd never bothered to inform the navy of his career change.

As we approached Wichita, Kansas, Ronnie delved into his biggest regret. In 1983, the navy finally tracked him down and arrested him at a poker table, right in the middle of a hand. He would later laugh and claim, "The players never even bothered to look up to see me dragged away in cuffs."

After a few months of jail time, and forfeiture of his meager navy salary, Ronnie was released with a less than honorable discharge from the military and stripped of his veteran's benefits. He returned to Vegas to resume his life as a dealer, but his sheriff's card—the identification card necessary to work in the casino industry in the state of Nevada—had been voided. His

---

* *Cold deck*—another name for *cooler*, a prearranged deck that is secretly switched into play. Can also be used as a verb. To *cold-deck a game* is to switch in a *cooler*.

past had caught up to him, and that brush with the authorities was enough to end his career in the casinos.

He told me, "Going AWOL was the biggest mistake of my life." There wasn't much time for regrets, though. He still needed to eat and send money back home. So he moved back to Tennessee and returned to playing in low-stakes private card games. The second half of the '80s were tough for Ronnie. After years of working with and *for* others, he was truly on his own.

Ronnie's story was placed on pause when we reached our first major stop on the trip, Kansas City, where we met his old buddy TJ, a gaunt man with a pockmarked face, who must have been in his early seventies.

The sun was coming up as we parked in the gravel driveway of a charming ranch house. TJ opened the screen door and greeted us on the porch wearing overalls. He introduced us to his "better half," a silver-haired woman with horn-rimmed glasses, who insisted on serving us coffee.

I sat there listening to the two old friends catch up. They gossiped about a crooked acquaintance who had been caught by the police and lamented the passing of another friend. But Ronnie had not come there only to reminisce and gossip. Before too long, he asked, "So I hear you got something special to show me?"

"That I do," TJ said. He finished his coffee and led us to his garage out back. I tingled with anticipation as he removed the padlock on the garage door, which he then insisted on lifting himself. Inside, it looked like any other workstation used by machinists and woodworkers, dominated by large mechanical devices with various drill bits and saw blades. Little jars of white paint lined the shelves above the workbench, along with cups jammed full with brushes. The floor was littered with crumpled pieces of sandpaper, iron filings, scraps of gold foil, and what appeared to be red sawdust. I stared at the evidence, trying to decipher what TJ did for a living.

"You mind giving the kid a demo?" Ronnie asked him, gesturing to the machinery.

"Oh, I think we can manage," TJ replied. Then he picked up a brick made of shiny red plastic. He set the brick on a machine that had a thin saw blade. As TJ fired up the contraption, Ronnie nudged me, encouraging me to get closer. He wanted me to watch the master at work.

I stood there, watching over the old man's shoulder as he sliced through the red brick. As he sliced off a smaller chunk, I realized what I was witnessing: TJ was a dice-maker. He was making loaded dice.

He cut and polished the cubes he'd created, then drilled holes where the white spots would soon be. Wearing jeweler's glasses, he measured tiny lead weights on a brass scale. Using tweezers, he inserted the lead into the dice. He sealed the weights into the cubes using a hot iron, then gave the brand-new dice a few rolls on the table, testing them, before painting the white spots onto each of the six sides.

TJ asked, "You want a stamp on these?" and opened a drawer that was full of metal letters and words I couldn't make out because they were backward. I didn't understand the question, but Ronnie did, answering, "Nah."

"Stamp?" I asked.

As TJ focused on the task at hand, Ronnie explained: Every casino brands its dice using a unique hot stamp, like a branding iron, and colored foil, usually gold or silver. These aren't just custom logos, they are an important measure to prevent cheaters from switching *their* crooked dice into the game. Unfortunately for the casinos, TJ had duplicates of every casino stamp in the country.

As we let the dice dry, TJ demonstrated the "juice joint," an electromagnet that can be concealed within a table and is used to activate magnetic dice (also known as "mags"). TJ handed me a pair of dice that appeared to be from the Bellagio casino, pointed to the opposite end of the long table, and said, "Aim just above the trim on the wall and give 'em a few tosses to make sure they are legit."

I rolled the dice a few times. Each time, Ronnie tossed them back to me from the other end of the table. Then TJ said, "Seem fair?"

"Fair," I said.

"All right, practice is over," TJ said, adding, "This is your come-out roll. You wanna win or you wanna lose?"

"Win," I said.

"Give 'em a roll."

I tossed the dice to the other end of the table. They landed: a five and a two. Winner.

TJ then explained that, unlike loaded dice, the mags could roll like normal dice (or "fronts"), until the operator pressed the secret button on the table, activating the electromagnet, causing the dice to favor certain numbers.

Then came the "special something" Ronnie had alluded to earlier. The three of us gathered around a black tarp that concealed a mystery object. TJ said, "You ready?" We were.

He pulled back the tarp to reveal what appeared to be a regulation casino roulette wheel, a circle of polished wood the size of a manhole cover. It had thirty-eight pockets (eighteen red, eighteen black, and two greens, 0 and 00) for the little white ball to randomly drop into.

TJ explained that his daughter had introduced him to a relatively new website called "eBay," which he regularly scoured for gambling devices. He had stumbled upon the listing for the wheel, which was in fine condition and reasonably priced. But when TJ looked at the cost of shipping, it was outrageous. So he checked the weight of the wheel and it was three times what it should have been. On a hunch, he bought the wheel and crossed his fingers.

TJ knelt down and gripped the wheel at its edges. He twisted the top as one would a lid on a giant jar, then lifted the top as he stood up, revealing the source of all that extra weight: Each of the thirty-six numbers was rigged with its own electromagnet. Each had its own set of red and black wires, all connected to separate batteries that were soldered to the interior wall of the wheel's outer rim. It was something out of a James Bond movie.

I didn't want to overreact; for all I knew these were common. Then I looked up and saw Ronnie's jaw on the floor. TJ said he had heard a rumor that this sort of thing existed but had never actually seen one. Now he owned one and, as if it were a classic car, he was going to fix it up and sell it for a pretty penny.

We congratulated TJ, made a bit more small talk, and thanked him for his hospitality. Then we hit the road again. As we drove off the property, down the gravel road, Ronnie said, "You almost forgot these," handing me the loaded dice I'd watched TJ make.

"I didn't pay for these!" I said, panicked, thinking I had mistaken what was meant to be a transaction for a free demonstration.

"Relax, they're yours. TJ wanted you to have them."

I said, "Thank you," then stared at my new treasure. We returned to the highway, and Ronnie continued telling me the story of his past.

By the early 1990s, he had found a new groove as a mechanic for hire, posing as a dealer the way he did in Vegas, but for private games all over the world. He dealt for an oil tycoon in Texas, who refused to lose to his wealthy poker pals. Ronnie helped a Hollywood actor fleece rich friends in a "friendly game." And he dealt for athletes, primarily basketball players. Names anyone would recognize, even if they'd never followed the sport.

Not all of his games were glamorous. At one point he found himself dealing poker for the biggest drug dealer in Atlanta, and counted no fewer than three AK-47s in the room during a preliminary meeting. Although none of the guns was pointed directly at him, the implications of what would happen to him if he screwed up or attempted to double-cross his "employer" were quite clear.

Our next stop was St. Louis. We went to a diner under an over-pass, at 1:00 a.m. Ronnie and I sat in a booth toward the back. As we struggled to drink our thick vanilla milkshakes through our straws, a man Ronnie called "the Doctor" walked in.

He was a pensive Filipino gentleman with streaks of silver in his jet-black hair. I remember thinking he dressed like he worked in the NASA control room, wearing a short-sleeved button-down shirt with a notepad and pencils protruding from the pocket.

He joined us at our booth, said, "Hey," to Ronnie. Refer-ring to me, he said, "Who's this?" Ronnie had known the guy for years, but their relationship was clearly more business than pleasure.

"I told you I was bringing a friend," Ronnie said.

"You didn't tell me it was a kid," he said, as if I weren't sitting there.

To put the guy at ease, Ronnie looked at me and said, "Show him something."

I knew the drill. I pushed aside the silverware and used my napkin to wipe up the ring of water my cup left behind. Then I shuffled and cut the cards three times. With each cut, I found an ace, which I tossed aside. When the fourth and final ace hit the table, Ronnie looked at the Doctor and said, "Need to see more?"

He'd seen enough.

We paid the check, got in our car, and followed the Doctor back to his office, which was in a quiet neighborhood with wide streets and houses that all looked identical. The Doctor pulled into one of the driveways and we parked across the street. Before we got out of the car I said, "I thought we were going to his office?" Ronnie replied, "We are. It's in the dude's basement."

The Doctor requested that we take our shoes off and leave them at the door. We entered the house, but for some reason the Doctor didn't turn any lights on. So we blindly followed his silhouette through the house until we reached the basement door. Thankfully, he turned on the light over the staircase leading down. From the top of the stairs, you could see the concrete floor of the basement.

The Doctor went down and Ronnie followed, using the yellow walls to keep his balance. As I descended, the room revealed itself. To the right, stacks and stacks of newspapers occupied an entire wall. A lonely recliner sat across from a depressingly old TV. Directly in front of me, a wooden dining table had been repurposed as a makeshift workstation, covered with hundreds of decks of playing cards, tinctures of ink, and what appeared to be a set of night-vision goggles. To the left was a grimy countertop with a hot plate and scale, alongside various powders and liquids in glass jars. Depending on your perspective, it looked like a sad science room or an exquisite meth lab.

The Doctor handed me a deck of cards and encouraged me to examine all of them, saying, "Look, look." As I examined them, front and back, he asked, "What do you see?"

I saw nothing out of the ordinary and told him so.

Then the Doctor said, "Now put these on," handing me a pair of ordinary-looking wire-framed reading glasses. I put the spectacles on, looked down at the cards, and couldn't believe my eyes. Peering through the lenses, I could see that the markings on the cards were now visible and clear as day. On the back of the Queen of Hearts were a *Q* and an *H* that could easily be read from ten, even twenty feet away.

The Doctor was an optometrist who subsidized his income by making marked cards. His marks were invisible to the human eye; he also created the special optical devices to read them. He was a man with a singular obsession: He wanted X-ray vision.

Like me, he had developed an obsession during his adolescence. It began when he ordered a pair of X-ray specs from the back of a comic book. The ad promised *AMAZING X-RAY VISION INSTANTLY!* With a power like that, he could rule the world. Weeks later, he received a pair of plastic frames with cardboard disks that had tiny holes for lenses. He felt shafted, but the seed was planted. He wanted the glasses he had imagined and spent his entire life trying to make them.

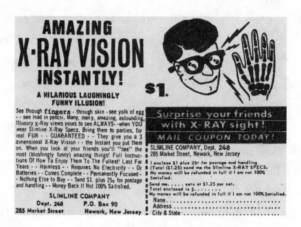

I was blown away by his work. I was certainly aware of the concept of infrared ink, markings that were invisible to the naked eye, but I also knew you had to wear suspicious dark sunglasses to read them. This was something else. The Doctor had developed his own formula for ink and had designed crystal-clear lenses that looked as innocent as your father's reading glasses.

After that, the Doctor showed us the camera system he had built to read the same markings. He showed us the blueprints for the latest peek store[*] he'd designed for a high-stakes private game in Macao. Then he pressed the Play button on his VCR and showed us footage of the system being tested: grainy green-and-black footage, shot directly above a card table. The dealer

---

[*] *Peek store*—a game designed to secretly glimpse at card players' hands. That information is then discreetly relayed (via hand signals or a "thumper," an electronic device that straps to your leg and delivers signals through taps or vibrations) to a confederate seated at that table.

sailed cards to players around the table, only the tops of their heads visible. It would have looked like typical security footage were it not for the purple glowing letters and numbers on the backs of the playing cards.

The more the Doctor shared his creations, the more he warmed up to us. I could tell he was enjoying how much I appreciated his work. And rightfully so; this was one of the few times in his life when the man was able to show off his creations to an adoring audience. Little did I know it was all a buildup to the main event.

The Doctor now showed us what Ronnie had gone there to see. First he set a pack of cigarettes on the workbench. Then he handed Ronnie a deck of cards and instructed him to shuffle, saying, "Imagine we're playing hold'em and you're the dealer."

As Ronnie shuffled, the Doctor asked me, "How many players?"

He was asking me to tell him how many players were sitting at our imaginary game. I said, "Seven."

"When you're done shuffling, place the cards here, to let me cut them." He gestured to the spot in front of him, near the pack of cigarettes. The Doctor cut the cards and said, "Now deal."

Ronnie dealt seven hands to the imaginary players.

Then the Doctor quietly said, "The flop will be Four of Diamonds, Ten of Spades, King of Clubs."

Ronnie burned a card,* then dealt the flop: Four of Diamonds. Ten of Spades. King of Clubs.

---

* *Burn a card*—to set a card aside (facedown) at the beginning of a round, before any other cards are dealt. This card is not used or seen by any player.

I was stunned and it showed. Ronnie was absolutely stone-faced.

The Doctor asked, "Want to know the turn and the river?"

I sure as hell did, but Ronnie calmly said, "I've seen enough."

The Doctor shrugged, then proceeded to show us the mechanics behind the miracle. The cards were marked, but not on the backs as was usually done. Instead, they were marked on their thin edges, in essence creating an invisible bar code along the edge of the entire deck.

The pack of cigarettes contained a tiny camera that scanned the bar code and transmitted the image to a cell phone he had in his pocket. The software he'd created instantly calculated the order of the cards and, silently cuing him with coded vibrations, gave him the identities of the cards being dealt.

In other words, he had built a system that could determine the position of every single playing card in a shuffled deck of cards. It could tell you who was going to win every hand before a single card was ever dealt. It was a time machine that allowed him to peer into the future of the game. Best of all, what used to take an entire building and a team of people now fit into the pocket of one single person.

Ronnie remained impassive. I couldn't tell if he was playing it cool because he had seen it before or if he didn't want to give the guy the satisfaction. His cold reaction made the humorless

---

The main reason for this procedure is to guard against marked cards. If the cards are marked, a cheater who can read the backs will know what the top card on the deck is. Burning the top card renders that knowledge useless.

Doctor awkward enough to crack a joke, saying, "You get one of these and you can give your hands a rest."

As Ronnie stared at the pack of cigarettes on the table, it all clicked into focus for me. I understood why Ronnie wasn't impressed. He had known about this device, but he had never seen one in person. That's why we were there: Ronnie wanted to come face-to-face with his replacement.

By the time I met Ronnie, these little devices were already circulating in the gambling world and he could feel the impact. His phone rang less and less. One by one, his former employers had the same realization: Instead of paying top dollar for a world-class card sharp, they could pay a onetime fee and have a device they could train any idiot to use. Or even do it themselves. You don't need to split the take with a computer.

Ronnie asked the Doctor, "How much?"

"Five thousand."

Ronnie shook his head and said, "I'm gonna need to think about it."

I was surprised to hear he was even considering it. Sure, five grand was a small investment considering he'd easily make the money back in one night. And using that little device was certainly safer than executing sleight-of-hand under watchful eyes. But when it came to being a crook, Ronnie was a purist. It was never *just* about getting the money; it also mattered *how* he got it. To him, using a fancy gadget like that was—as peculiar as it sounds—cheating. And, despite the nefarious nature of the business, he believed there was dignity in earning a living with your own hands.

Unfortunately, dignity didn't pay the bills. The world around him was evolving and he needed to stay relevant.

Later in the trip, I learned Ronnie had already begun supplementing his income. I'm not sure he would have told me, had he not made a joke I didn't understand, saying, "I'm tired of paying my rent in quarters." When I asked him what that meant, I could see by the look on his face that he'd forgotten I didn't already know. With an embarrassed sigh, he proceeded to tell me what he'd been up to in the past few months.

A friend of Ronnie's had introduced him to a device used to steal money from slot machines, called a "light wand." It was nothing more than a piece of sturdy wire, roughly the length of a pencil, with a 9-volt battery attached to one end and a tiny Christmas-tree bulb soldered to the other. This crude little device was capable of emptying a slot machine in a matter of minutes. Back then, the way a slot machine paid the players was by allowing coins to roll down a ramp, passing them in between a built-in light source and a small optical sensor. As each coin rolled past the slot machine's internal light, its shadow was cast onto the sensor. The sensor "saw" the shadow and recognized that a coin had been paid to the player. The light wand effectively blinded the machine. The device was snaked up through the coin hopper, positioning the little bulb near the machine's optic sensor. Once in position, the cheater pressed the CASH OUT button and coins rolled down the ramp, but the light wand prevented any shadows from being cast onto the sensor. Unable to recognize the shadows, the machine did not register the coins leaving the machine and it continued dispensing them until the machine was empty.

Ronnie's friend was excited about the light wand but too scared to use it. Ronnie wasn't. He mastered the device in only a few hours, capable of emptying a machine of close to a thousand dollars in coins in a matter of minutes. And since Vegas was a "target-rich" town, Ronnie didn't need to risk using the device in casinos with their multimillion-dollar security systems. Instead, he hit the slots at every convenience store, Laundromat, and twenty-four-hour pancake house in town.

Had someone just told me they robbed banks to pay their bills, I would have gotten out of the car at the next stop and hitchhiked home. But I never judged Ronnie for doing what he needed to do to survive. He judged himself plenty.

Ronnie wasn't proud of his mastery of the light wand, because it required more chutzpah than talent. It wasn't cheating, it was just theft, and he knew the difference. It's a strange distinction to make, but I understood it. I never heard him sound ashamed until he talked about robbing the slot machines. He made light of it, saying, "I've gotta commit ten felonies a month just to pay the rent!" It was meant to be funny, but it wasn't far from the truth.

The majority of our trip was scored by jazz music. Ronnie kept a CD case loaded with all his favorites. He "introduced" me to Charlie Parker, Thelonious Monk, and Miles Davis. As we listened, he dissected their music as if it were conceptual art.

Most of what he described seemed abstract, saying things that were beyond my comprehension at that time, like "It's not about the notes they play, it's about the notes they don't play." He also used the word "it" a lot when trying to describe the music. He'd say things like "He really knew how to find *it*." Or "Miles knew how to put *it* into every note." And he told me, "You gotta hear *it* before you can play *it*."

I couldn't hear *it*. But I wanted to. And if studying sleight-of-hand had taught me anything, it was to appreciate the things I couldn't see. I figured the same applied to what I wasn't hearing. I was determined to keep listening, and at some point I realized that Ronnie talked about musicians the way I talked about Ronnie. The feelings he described while listening to jazz musicians were exactly how I felt when I watched him handle a deck of cards.

There was nothing frivolous about Ronnie's work. It wasn't just that he was technically brilliant (he was), but there was a gravity to his work that I didn't see in the hands of any of the magicians I had studied. When Ronnie touched the cards, it *meant* something. He knew how to find *it* and he put *it* into the cards.

By the time we reached Knoxville, I felt like I really knew Ronnie. That connection solidified when he showed me his old neighborhood, the high school he'd gone to, the apartment complex where his childhood home used to be, and the intersection where his older brother died.

My last night on our trip, the night before I had to head to the airport, he took me to his favorite BBQ joint, where slabs of meat were served on paper plates, with sides of baked beans and corn bread.

As he finished his last rib, I asked Ronnie, "How did you know you were good enough to sit down that first time?"

He scoffed and reminded me that it wasn't a choice; his older brother had forced him into the life. Then I joked about him doing the same for me. He wiped the sauce off his fingers, leaned in to talk business, and asked, "You're thinking about getting into a game?"

"I've been thinking about it," I said, impersonating a badass. He chuckled.

"What?" I asked, wanting to clarify what was so fucking funny.

"Are you serious?" he asked.

When I told him I was, his demeanor changed. He stared at me for a moment. It was the same look my mother gave me after I confessed to concealing the five-dollar bill from her. But, unlike my mother, he didn't offer poetic wisdom like "Be the light." Instead, he tossed his napkin on his plate and said, "Let's go."

The parking lot, lit by a single streetlamp, was mostly vacant. Before we got to the car, Ronnie stopped and said, "I want you to see something." Then he turned around and lifted his T-shirt, revealing his back to me. Along the right side, scattered from his hip to his shoulder blade, were seven scars. I stared at the marks as Ronnie explained their origin:

In the late '80s, after he lost his cozy gig as the bust-out dealer in Vegas, Ronnie found himself scraping by with any card game he could find. One night, in the back of a bar, he cheated some strangers out of a couple hundred bucks. After the game, as he was walking home, the players caught up to him, pinned him against a car, and stabbed him seven times with a four-inch blade.

Lowering his shirt, he said, "I don't even know if those motherfuckers jumped me because they thought I was cheatin' or if they just wanted their money back." This was Ronnie's less-than-subtle way of revealing the world he had been shielding me from.

I had created a fiction for myself. I watched movies like *The Cincinnati Kid* and *The Sting* as if they were documentaries. I swallowed glorified stories about charismatic hustlers like Titanic Thompson. Then, with Ronnie, I got to hang out in pool halls, meet eccentric characters, and learn their secrets. But movies aren't real life. Books are written by authors with agendas. And while Ronnie *was* as complex and cool as any character from *Ocean's Eleven*, he kept the uglier truths hidden from me, until he couldn't.

He made it clear from the beginning: He never would have given me the time of day if he thought I was going to follow in his footsteps. While I may have forgotten that I was a tourist in his world, Ronnie never did. He put it into perspective when he asked, "Why the hell would you *choose* this life?" The moment he said it, I recognized that I was asking to enter a world he would have given anything to escape. I was embarrassed and ashamed. I never asked again.

I didn't know where things stood between us until he took me to the airport the following day. We weren't allowed to park at the curb, so I grabbed my bag from the trunk while Ronnie kept the car running. I closed the trunk, walked around to the passenger side, and leaned down through the window to say farewell. Before I could say anything, he handed me a small paper bag and said, "Don't open this until you get inside." I shook his hand, thanked him for the mystery bag and again for the trip, then said goodbye.

Ronnie drove off as I walked into the terminal. The moment I passed through the doors I looked in the bag to find a Post-it that read: *Thanks for the company.* Then I almost fell over when I saw the gift itself: the lead-filled walnut, once carried— but never thrown—by Titanic Thompson himself. My very own gobstopper.

Ronnie and I spoke often over the next few years. Then one day the calls stopped. I found out through a friend that Ronnie had been arrested. One of the world's greatest sleight-of-hand artists got busted for robbing a slot machine in the back of a convenience store in Las Vegas. It was so fucking humiliating for him.

Ronnie couldn't avoid jail time for his conviction. He was sent to a state prison just north of Vegas. We became pen pals. Keeping his sense of humor, he signed all of his letters from prison, *Wish you were here!*

SEVEN YEARS IN A DAY

I heard the hum of the fan before I felt the breeze on my arm. I tried to open my eyes, but I couldn't. It felt like someone had sealed them shut with superglue while I was sleeping. I ordered my hands to help, but they disobeyed the command. Then I tried to kick the sheet and blanket off of me and nothing happened. I couldn't even call for help. It was a mutiny of my own body.

I couldn't move a single muscle, yet I was totally aware of the world around me. It was so surreal, for a moment I thought I was merely *dreaming* that I was awake. But when I heard the garbage truck outside my window, I had a profoundly terrifying realization: I was conscious, but my mind was completely disconnected from my body. That's when panic set in.

If someone were to have seen me lying there, it would have looked as though I was peacefully sleeping. But inside I was screaming, pleading with my body, begging it to move. The more I struggled, the more dread I felt. My thoughts continued clawing at the walls of my mind until I realized *there were no walls of my mind*. I was trying to escape, but from what? There was no lock to pick because there was no door to open. Nor were there bars to squeeze through or a floor to dig up. I was trapped in nothing and there was no escape.

Realizing my own thoughts were the cause of my fear and anxiety, I stopped struggling. I embraced the void, allowing the darkness to swallow me whole. A calmness set in and I fell back asleep. But only for a second. The moment my mind dozed off, it instantly reconnected with my body. My eyes sprung open and I flung myself out of bed. I was free.

I was twenty-five years old and living in Los Angeles. I had never experienced sleep paralysis before that. It's a form of parasomnia, like sleepwalking or night terrors. It used to be viewed as a form of demonic possession, and understandably so; it remains one of the more terrifying experiences of my life.

It was also a terrible way to start a day when I had an important job interview. I *had* a job working as a production assistant at a company that made documentaries. It wasn't glamorous by any means, but I really enjoyed learning about filmmaking. In a sense, I was living the Hollywood dream, working in "the industry." Unfortunately, the partners hated each other and dismantled the company.

Before that, I'd worked as a file clerk at a law office in the San Fernando Valley. I organized documents, made copies, and did any menial task the lawyers asked me to do. But that abruptly ended when the owner of the firm fled the country after being indicted for embezzling money from clients.

When I first moved to LA I sold gym memberships and cell phones. Not at the same time. After those gigs didn't pan out, I worked at a movie theater, tearing tickets and making popcorn. I left that job when the Scientologist owners began indoctrinating their employees.

At one point, I waited tables. I had heard servers made good money, but I didn't have any experience. So I started as a busboy and, after a few months, got promoted to waiter. For some strange reason, after I was promoted, the manager kept telling me to shave, even after I already had. I'd shave when I woke up. A few hours later I'd roll in to work. The manager would look at me and say, "How many times do I have to tell you to shave before your shift?" One day he actually made me purchase a disposable razor from the convenience store across the street. "Go shave!" he ordered. I couldn't understand what the hell he was talking about, but he was my boss so I did what he said. When

I returned from the store with a disposable blade, I passed by him and held it up, making sure he saw me take it into the restroom. Once in there, I *didn't* shave. Instead I just splashed some water on my face, waited a few minutes, and then went back to my manager, asking, "Better?" When he replied, "Much," I quit.

I was so tired of fluttering from job to job. I wanted a career. After weeks of submitting applications all around town, I finally landed an interview with another, much larger production company than the one I had worked at. With only fifty bucks left in my bank account, I desperately needed it to go well.

My phone rang as I was getting dressed. It was Vanessa, calling to make sure I didn't sleep through my alarm.

An intelligent porcelain beauty with no patience for bullshit, Vanessa was the only constant in my life. The first time I saw her she was dangling from a tall tree, coiled in a long piece of red fabric, practicing aerial acrobatics. Like me, she was an only child, raised by a single mother. Our broken pieces fit nicely together.

We had moved in together after dating for a year. Our humble apartment was two blocks from the movie theater where celebrities immortalize their hands in cement. Unlike me, Vanessa was responsible and hardworking, two of the many admirable traits she did not inherit from her mother, who at sixty years old was still trying to make it as an actress.

Most days, she woke up hours before me to go to a stuffy office building where she worked with wolves that had migrated west from Wall Street. After work, she'd spend an hour in traffic and get home just in time to get ready for her *second* job, managing a nightclub in Hollywood. In other words, between the two of us, we had two jobs.

I was hoping to change that this day.

My interview was held at "Nakatomi Plaza," the skyscraper from the movie *Die Hard*. The man interviewing me was serious but polite. Things were going well until he asked, "Where'd you go to college?"

"I didn't go to college," I said. Then, correcting myself, "Actually, I took some college classes, but that was only to graduate from high school."

That's where I lost him. And the job. He bluntly stated that they were looking for someone with a college degree. At which point I thanked him for his time and then left with my tail between my legs.

I had only briefly considered attending a university. After my road trip with Ronnie. Seeing the scars on his back was a reality check. I had spent my adolescence staring at my hands. I finally looked up to see life hurtling toward me and I was wholly unprepared.

My grades were uneven. There was an entire year that was mysteriously missing from the timeline, and there were asterisks by the credits I had earned outside of high school. Even if I got accepted, I didn't know how to pay for it. Neither I nor my mother had any savings. I had no idea where to get a grant, and the idea of going into debt with student loans terrified me. Without knowing what I wanted to study, it all sounded like a bad bet.

As I drove home from the interview, the heavy traffic gave me plenty of time to feel sorry for myself. I was disappointed that I didn't have better news for Vanessa. At home I told her, "Another swing and a miss."

"It's okay, it wasn't meant to be," she said, adding, "You'll get the next one."

She had more faith in me than I did. But I wanted to believe like she did, so I agreed.

Then she kissed me and said, "Ready to go?"

"Go?"

I had completely forgotten we had plans. And it was the last place I wanted to go.

A few times a year, I would accompany Vanessa to one of her corporate office parties. She would spend most of the evening making sure her boss was having a good time. That meant *my* evening was spent avoiding small talk with her coworkers, who were mostly handsome guys my age, fresh out of their Ivy League schools and already making six figures.

The shindig was on the rooftop of a swank hotel. Vanessa introduced me to new faces right before her boss spotted her and summoned her over. I found myself listening to guys compare their Rolexes. I owned a Casio watch and never wore it, so I had little to contribute to the conversation.

Then, to my surprise, one of them said, "So, Vanessa tells me you're a magician?"

I replied, "I used to be. Sort of. But not anymore." Then, to avoid any follow-up questions, I immediately excused myself from the circle.

After ruling out college, back when I was still living in Colorado, pursuing a career as a professional magician seemed, ironically, like the responsible thing to do. I had already invested seven years into it. All I needed to do was resolve my bizarre aversion to performing.

Walt was convinced it was performance anxiety. He said the only cure was "flight time." I just needed to start performing. So I did.

But there were so few opportunities that I cold-called places and offered my services, free of charge. One out of twenty would say yes. When Mom heard I was looking for venues, she had me perform at every firehouse in the Springs.

I began to think the magic shop might be holding me back. It had served me well, but it was time to move on. Walt understood. He knew I couldn't work there forever, not with what he paid. I still visited often. Walt and I continued to hang out. The day I went to turn in my keys to the shop, Walt said, "Keep 'em."

I still saw Walt regularly and he sent gigs my way. When people called the shop looking to hire a magician, he'd give them my number. These gigs were far from glamorous: I wowed the folks at the retirement home. I dazzled them at the sweet-sixteen party in the back of a pizza parlor. I even shared a few miracles with the sinners at the local church.

But the flight time didn't help. After a year of performing, I had gotten better, but I still wasn't enjoying it.

A friend suggested I study theater, pointed me to some acting classes offered by the local theater company. Made sense; I had spent time performing, but I hadn't invested any time *learning how to perform*. I was desperate to unlock my inner showman.

It was a one-month summer course. On day one I was given a monologue to recite on day two. I got up in front of the class and, to my surprise, didn't feel any of the apprehension I had always felt when performing magic. In fact, I found it enjoyable.

After the end of the program, the director asked me to be in the next play they were putting on for the public. I played a Mormon named "Rick" who kills himself after being seduced by a gay con artist. Even got a decent review in the local paper. Never once was I uncomfortable onstage, not even on opening night.

After the play, I thought I might be cured of the discomfort I had felt while conjuring. I got to test that theory at my very next gig, working in the lounge at a golf club, but that same familiar dread returned the moment I booked the job. Whatever it was that was burdening me, it was specific to being a magician.

Not long after, Walt called to tell me that the great conjuror Grayson was returning to the ritzy Broadmoor Hotel for another private show. But this time, not only did he invite Walt *and me* to join him for drinks, he invited us to attend his actual performance.

I was thrilled to see Grayson again, but this was an especially prodigious moment for me. *Seven years* after buying my first magic book, I was finally going to see a proper magic show. I had watched a magician perform on a small stage at a state fair. I had seen a street busker in Boulder, but he spent most of the show gathering a crowd and soliciting tips. And, in Aspen, I had watched a bar magician astonish tourists in between serving libations. But I had never actually seen a show where people showed up, faced in the same direction, and did nothing but watch a magician for more than an hour. Much less one of the greatest magicians in the world. If anything was going to inspire me to embrace performing, it was seeing Grayson go toe-to-toe with an audience.

At the Broadmoor, the ready-made theater was in the presidential suite at the end of a majestic hallway. The room was filled with row after row of wooden chairs, all facing a round table, which was covered with a black cloth, a chair on each side. Classical music underscored the chatter in the air.

Walt and I did our best to look like we could afford to be there, but it wasn't easy. Even though we were guests of the performer, we felt like imposters in our cheap suits, surrounded by the beau monde. So, as the other guests took their seats, we stood in the back of the room, staring out the large windows that framed the sun as it reflected on a lake before vanishing behind the snow-capped mountains. After everyone was seated, the music faded down, the room darkened, and Grayson entered.

He was wearing a bespoke gray three-piece with the same black fedora he'd had on when I first met him, which he placed on the table. His salt-and-pepper hair was neatly combed at the beginning of the evening but would become increasingly disheveled as the performance intensified. And he was shorter than I had remembered; but his presence was even more commanding.

Once in front of the expectant crowd, Grayson looked at

us, soaking us in, and then, with a deep voice, he said, "Good evening." As he continued his introduction, I marveled at his sophistication and eloquence, not a hint of pretention. He was the opposite of the cheesy clichés we've come to think of when we think of magicians.

Then, using only a pack of playing cards and a few objects borrowed from the audience, Grayson proceeded to pummel the crowd with wonderfully unnatural events: Cards danced between his hands. He caused a wedding band to vanish and then appear in the center of an ice cube. He produced a dozen lemons from a lady's purse. I would say he was performing "classic" tricks, but he's the one who invented them.

The crowd was loving it. So was I. But then something unexpected occurred.

Grayson placed a small wooden box on the table. He said his father had given it to him when he was a boy, but there was a condition. "My father told me I mustn't open the box until he died," Grayson said with conviction. Then, placing his hand on the box as if it were his prized possession, Grayson went on to say, "It would be another fifteen years before my father passed. I'd like to show you what I discovered that day . . ."

His words began to cast a fog over the joy and wonder I was feeling. As he continued speaking, the fog thickened, clouding my experience. By the time Grayson asked for a volunteer from the audience, all I felt was nothing as I had the thought: *That's not true.*

I had seen that box before, on one of Walt's tapes. Grayson had performed this same routine, with that exact same box, in the '80s. Only that's not what he said back then. On the tape, Grayson claimed the box had been given to him by a holy man in Tibet. It seemed he'd changed the script to bolster the effect and give it some theatricality.

The story about his father was effective, and Grayson told it well. But as the crowd was on the edge of their seats, mesmerized, the same thought echoed through the fog in my mind over and over again: *That's not true.*

At the conclusion of the routine, when the crowd applauded, I had to remind myself to clap along with them. As Grayson continued on with the show, I tried to shake the heavy fog that had come over me, but I couldn't. Rather than appreciating Grayson's artistry, or allowing myself to simply be entertained, I spent the rest of the show focused on, dissecting, every lie he told.

None of the lies were harmful. They were theatrical untruths; little fibs here and there, used as both scaffolding and decoration for the experience. And the audience certainly didn't care if what he was saying was true or not. In fact, most of them probably assumed that *nothing* he said was true.

Karl Germain, the celebrated conjuror, known to the masses as Germain the Wizard, famously said, "Magic is the only honest profession. A magician promises to deceive you and then he does." In this respect, Grayson was the most honest man I'd ever seen take the stage. Knowing he was the best of the best, right there in the middle of his show, I came to the uncomfortable realization:

I'm not interested in deceiving people.

It was as if I had devoted my life to playing the cello, and, in the midst of watching Yo-Yo Ma play live for the first time, I realized I didn't even want to be a musician. I wanted to get up and walk out of the room right then and there. But I had too much respect for Grayson and Walt. So I sat there experiencing a hurricane of emotions.

After the show, Grayson received a well-deserved standing ovation. I did my best to put on a smile, but it wasn't convincing enough, because after the applause died down, Walt turned to me and asked, "Are you okay?"

I told him I wasn't feeling well and that I should probably go. We were supposed to have dinner with the maestro, but I had to get out of there. Walt said, "At least say hi to Grayson." But I couldn't. Not even for Walt. I told him to thank Grayson for the show and took a cab home.

Once home, I picked up my journal and attempted to unpack the revelation. A stream of consciousness poured through my pen and onto the page.

I am not interested in fooling people. Or at least that's why I'm so uncomfortable performing as a magician. It's not about deception. It's about the deception of truth. To know illusions is to know reality. How can we know what's true if we can't recognize what's false?

I went on to confront my own hypocrisy, asking: *I'm not a gay Mormon, how is magic different?*

Out of context, that's a pretty fantastic question. But I was referring to the play I had acted in, where I played Rick, the gay Mormon. I stood on a stage, presenting myself as someone I wasn't, saying things that didn't actually happen. How were those lies different from Grayson's when he claimed he inherited the box from his father? Or when I first met Walt, and he told me the story about his white pocketknife? I was challenging myself to explain the difference between the lies told in a stage play and those uttered in a magic show.

My answer was mostly rubbish, but I summed it up succinctly:

Both [the play and the magic show] present illusions. But the play uses its illusions to point to larger truths. The magic show points to itself. The magician keeps the audience focused on the illusion. Deception is the point. What truth does deception for deception's sake reveal? That we can be deceived? That's not enough.

In the margins, I wrote: *Orson Welles didn't want to be a magician. He wanted to be a MAGICIAN.*

My fascination with Mr. Welles had begun when I was young and someone remarked that we shared the same birthday, May 6. I watched his films, listened to his radio shows. I knew that he was interested in magic from seeing *F for Fake*. But it wasn't until I saw a series of clips of Orson performing stage illusions on one of Walt's VHS tapes that I realized he was an accomplished conjuror. Then I learned that he had practiced and performed magic his entire life: As a boy he learned tricks from Houdini; he performed at friends' birthday parties, even more so after he was famous. At the end of his life he created a full stage show called *Orson Welles' Magic Show*, which he filmed but died before finishing.

Before he died, Orson was asked, "Mr. Welles, you're an accomplished director, writer, producer, a star of radio, stage, and screen. When you're gone, how would you like to be remembered?"

Orson replied, "As a *magician*."

When I heard him give that answer, knowing his lifelong love of magic, I took it at face value. Years later, seeing Grayson's show, I realized that I had misunderstood. Orson didn't want to be remembered as a trickster or even a supreme illusionist. He wanted to be remembered as a *real magician*, someone who revealed *more* than he concealed, someone who bridged the gap between our collective consciousness and the divine.

Knowing Orson Welles happened to *also* be a theatrical magician confused the issue for me. Had I heard Maya Angelou deliver the same answer, there would have been no confusion on my part. I would've known she was speaking metaphorically, metaphysically, spiritually.

I asked myself a question I'd never considered before:

What kind of magician do you want to be?

I rambled for a page. Then I bitterly scratched out what I had written and rewrote the question:

What kind of magician do you want to be?

Then I refused to place the pen to the paper until I had an answer that felt true. Eventually I wrote:

I want to be the prisoner that returns to the cave.
In Plato's story, the prisoner escapes and sees the outside world, then returns to the cave to release the other prisoners, only to be threatened by them. They call him mad and refuse to be freed.

That's where Plato's story ends. I imagined what came next . . .

The escapee doesn't abandon his former cellmates when they refuse to be freed. Those are his people down there and it's not their fault they can't accept the truth he's trying to show them. So rather than leaving the cave, the escapee picks up the tools of the puppeteer and teaches himself to cast shadows, with the hope of using those illusions to set the others free.

That's the type of magician I wanted to be.
But I didn't know how to do that.
Especially not as a magician.
I stopped performing. I stopped practicing. And if anyone had doubted my commitment to starting down a new path, I sold my once-prized collection of magic books and used the cash to move to Los Angeles.

———

Hours had passed at the bar atop the hotel. Vanessa found me sitting alone in a corner, eating shrimp cocktail, still sulking about losing the job I never had. I was relieved to hear her say, "We can go." In the car ride home, she tried to lift my spirits, telling me, "Everything happens for a reason."

At home I had trouble sleeping. The moment I lay down in bed I stopped thinking about the failed job interview and started thinking about how I'd begun the day trapped in my own body. I didn't want to experience that again. Ever.

Closing my eyes was an act of faith.

Then my phone rang.

Who the hell is calling at this hour?

I didn't recognize the number. "Hello?"

"Hey, it's Ronnie."

Vanessa, half asleep, muttered, "Everything okay?"

I told her, "Everything is fine, go back to sleep." Then I moved into the living room to take the call.

Ronnie and I had kept in touch over the years. He'd served two years in prison for robbing that slot machine. After he got out, I'd taken Vanessa to meet him in Vegas. The three of us had dinner, saw a Cirque du Soleil show, and then hung out at a pancake house, laughing until the sun came up. It had made me happy to see them get along so well.

I was excited to hear from my old friend. "Hey, man! How are you?"

"I'm surviving. How are you and the angel?"

I told him she was great and that I was getting by.

He dropped the small talk, saying, "Hey, listen. I'm in a jackpot."*

My heart sank. Last I knew, Ronnie had a job selling used cars in a parking lot under the scorching Vegas sun. It was long hours and the pay was terrible, but it was an honest living. As far as I knew, he'd been staying out of trouble and proud of the fact that he was cleaning up his act.

"What happened?" I asked.

"I got busted crossing the state line."

Ronnie wasn't supposed to leave the state of Nevada. So when the California Highway Patrol caught Ronnie driving with expired plates, they saw he was violating his parole and shipped him back to Nevada.

"Wait. What were you doing in California?"

"Working."

A year earlier, Ronnie was sweating out another day at the car lot, when a stranger approached him. The way Ronnie described it, it was as if the man appeared out of thin air. Ronnie showed him a white Cadillac with new rims. They got in the car, where the stranger dropped the charade. He wasn't there for a car; he was there for Ronnie.

The stranger made Ronnie a simple offer: *five thousand dollars to cheat one game in Los Angeles.* Ronnie was surprised. As far as he knew, people weren't hiring bust-out dealers anymore; they used fancy cameras and gadgets like the ones I'd seen in the Doctor's

---

* *Jackpot*—cheater slang for trouble with the law.

basement. The stranger told him that Ronnie was partially right. (In fact, the stranger himself had made a killing using technology.) But China had started mass-producing the gadgets and selling them online. Devices that were once impossible to find were suddenly available to anyone who googled "how to cheat at cards." The market was flooded with idiots using gadgets at tables, and the gaming world caught on to it. New security protocols were implemented. People started to wise up, learning how to check the cards for markings and recognize the devices.

Ronnie eloquently summarized what had happened, saying, "Dumb mothafuckas woke the dead."

But the stranger had come up with a new plan. In this modern era littered with technology, he believed the most reliable way to cheat was returning to the old ways. He wanted to hire someone to beat the game using sleight-of-hand. So he tracked down the last of a dying breed: Ronnie.

Ronnie didn't want to go back to that life. But he *couldn't* stay in the life he was living. With his record, selling cars was as decent a job as he'd ever find and he could barely afford to pay rent. It had been years since he could afford to send money to his family in Tennessee.

He agreed to deal the one game. It went so well, he dealt another. Before he knew it, he had quit his job at the car lot and was driving to Los Angeles once a week to deal cards at a big-money game in a fancy house in Beverly Hills.

Ronnie made it clear to me that his decision to start dealing again was centered around money and circumstances. But I figured it had to be more than that. The only time in his life he felt worth a damn was back in the '70s, working as a bust-out dealer for the casinos. That was the only time *others* had assigned value to him and his immense talent. Even though his role was secretive and nefarious, he felt as though he was a part of something special, which meant *he* was special.

The game in LA was a return to the good life. He made more than enough money to pay his bills and send money back home. And, considering previous experiences, it was relatively safe. He only had to commute from Vegas to LA once a week, and he enjoyed the drive. For the first time in as long as he could remember, he felt like he was worth a damn.

And then it all came crashing down. Ronnie was going back to jail for six months for violating his probation. Which meant the game that he had been dealing was shutting down. The stranger couldn't afford to keep the game running without Ronnie there to cheat it.

"Jesus, Ronnie, that's terrible," I said, lacking the proper condolences.

"Yeah," he said. Then he hesitated before saying, "So I was thinking maybe you'd fill in for me."

"What do you mean?"

"You deal the game until I get out."

I thought he was joking. When he started telling me how safe it was and how much money I could make, I realized he wasn't. He explained that if I worked as his "sub," they could keep the game rolling so it was still there for him when he was released.

"Why can't you just start it up again?" I asked.

He explained that it was a miracle they got players to show up in the first place. "Once they shut it down, it ain't ever coming back."

I didn't understand why he was asking *me*. He had made it very clear that he didn't want that life (his life) for me, and I believed him. My childish fantasies of cheating had evaporated the night Ronnie showed me his scars.

I said, "There's gotta be someone else who can help with this."

"I wouldn't be asking if there was."

"What about Pauly from Boston?"

"Arthritis locked up his hands."

"How about Moses? Or that guy from Detroit, the one you called 'Cracker Brian'?"

"Moses is dead and Cracker Brian won't return my calls."

I was speechless.

"You're it, kid," he said. Then he tipped his hand, saying, "If I can't keep this game going, I don't know what's gonna happen." His voice cracked; it sounded like he might be crying.

"Ronnie, what are you not telling me?"

Ronnie had successfully avoided seeing doctors most of his adult life. But when he was admitted to prison, he was given a physical exam. The doctor noticed Ronnie had some abdominal discomfort and ordered X-rays. Ronnie had colon cancer.

I couldn't believe it. You think heroes are bulletproof until Superman calls and asks you to save him.

Even *if* I wanted to help, I didn't know if I could. Since moving to LA, I had performed at a few nightclubs and done some private gigs to help pay the bills when money was really tight.

But other than that, I never touched cards. The last gig I had was before I worked at the law office, and that was a year and some months earlier.

Buying time to think it over, I asked, "Do I have to give you an answer right now?"

"Yes, 'cause once I hang up with you, I am making one more call to the boss to give him your answer. After that, I don't know when I'll get to talk on the phone again without someone listening in."

It was too much, too fast. I needed more time.

Knowing I was struggling, he said, "I'm sorry I'm asking you to do this." Then he said, "Look, you don't have to do anything yet. Just meet with them. If you don't feel good about it, walk away and never look back."

For all I knew, this could be the last time I would speak to Ronnie. I figured I could say yes to him now and then no to his boss later.

"When do they want to meet?" I asked.

"Tomorrow, two p.m."

I said, "Okay," and grabbed a pen and a pad.

I could hear the relief in his voice as he gave me the address. He thanked me and told me he'd make it up to me someday. Then he went on to tell me about the man who had hired him, Leo. He made it clear that Leo wasn't a card mechanic. He was a con man, hiring a mechanic to help him cheat.

Then he said, "So what name should I give them?"

"What do you mean?" I asked.

"What name do you wanna use?"

"What's wrong with my name?"

"Nothing. You wanna use your real name?"

"Well, not anymore. Why do I need an alias?"

"It's not an alias. It's just a precaution. What's your middle name?"

"Cody."

"Perfect."

The next morning, I told Vanessa about the call. She was saddened to hear about Ronnie's trouble with the law. She worried about him when I told her about his health. Then I told her about the game and that he'd asked me to fill in for him.

"What do you think?" I asked.

She replied, "I think you've already made up your mind."

WHAT *WAS* NORMAN ROCKWELL HIDING?

The CHECK ENGINE light on my dashboard was illuminated. It had been on for weeks and I couldn't understand why. I had checked the oil. The coolant was fine. It sounded fine; nothing rattled. Sure, it had 170,000 miles on it, but I was told that was nothing for a Honda. I wanted to have a mechanic look at it, but I couldn't afford to have it fixed, so what was the point? I just lived with it, and it hadn't bothered me when I was driving around the flatlands of Los Angeles. But as soon as I started up this steep winding road, all I could think about was how, at any moment, the engine was going to fall out and roll all the way back down the hill.

I was grateful to spot the address and parked on the gravel next to a tall, vine-covered wall. I walked toward the iron gate to enter the property as a Hollywood Star Tours van drove by, loaded with smiling tourists holding cameras. I wasn't sure what they expected to see, because all the houses in that neighborhood were buried in the woods or behind walls. Also, even *if* they saw a house, how would they know who really lived there? *Every house* in that neighborhood was a palace that could easily pass as a "celebrity home." It seemed less like a "star tour" and more like a traveling thought experiment: The driver, Schrödinger, points to a house and says, "Tom Hanks lives here." Then it's up to the observers to decide if that's true. The whole thing seemed like a racket.

Then again, who was I to judge?

I pressed the button on the keypad at the gate. A camera stared at me so I stared back. As I waited for someone on the other end to respond, I reconsidered what I was wearing. For a normal job interview I'd wear slacks and a button-down shirt, maybe even a pair of dress shoes. However, in those instances I was competing with other, more qualified candidates. Here I was their only shot; there literally were no other candidates. So I wore jeans, Converse sneakers, a T-shirt, and a hoodie, which I left in the car because it was too hot.

There was a buzz. The heavy gate slowly opened to reveal a sprawling driveway. A stone path cut through the green lawn, leading to the house itself: a two-story white Colonial with a black roof and a red front door. It looked like a Norman Rockwell painting. Knowing it was actually an illegal underground poker parlor made me wonder: *What* was *Norman Rockwell hiding?*

The front door opened when I was halfway up the path. A

silver-haired man with leathery limbs emerged, wearing a pink polo shirt and khaki shorts. I felt better seeing he was dressed even more casually than me.

He raised his hand to his eyes to block the sun, then squinted in my direction. As I got closer, I could see his puffy red face contort into a question mark.

"You Ronnie's friend?" He seemed puzzled by my appearance.

"Yes. Are you Leo?"

"I am."

He lowered his hand to shake mine with a firm grip. Bewildered, he asked, "How old are you?"

"Twenty-five," I said, realizing how little Ronnie must have told him.

He shrugged and led me inside. Beyond the marbled entryway I could see part of the living room. The floor and all the furniture were covered in plastic tarps. Just as I was thinking, *So this is how I die*, I was hit with the smell of fresh paint.

"Sorry about the mess. With Ronnie away, we thought we'd use the extra time to spruce the place up a bit," Leo said, closing the door behind me.

In the center, placed on top of a tarp, was a pristine poker table and some folding chairs. Leo sat down behind the empty chip tray.* He gestured to the flimsy chair across from him and said, "Take a seat."

---

* *Chip tray* (or *rack*)—a tray designed to hold poker chips in rows. It rests in the table in front of the dealer at the gaming table. This tray is removable and travels with its designated dealer.

He glanced at his watch as I sat down. Then he looked left and stared down a long hallway. I looked, expecting to see someone. After a few awkward beats with both of us staring at nothing, he looked at me and asked, "So how do you know Ronnie?"

I regaled him with a vague version of how Ronnie and I met. As I was telling the story, his eyes darted back to the long hallway. I turned to see an attractive brunette, wearing a tight dress, with tousled hair and smudged makeup. She crept past us like a lost woodland creature, carrying a pair of Louboutin heels.

Leo quietly muttered to himself, "What the hell?"

The two of us sat there, frozen, as she tiptoed through our clandestine meeting and then slipped out the front door.

A new voice down the hall asked, "Is she gone?"

Leo yelled, "What the fuck, Max?!"

A man around my age appeared wearing a pair of baggy jeans and nothing more. He was skinny but he walked with the strut of a bodybuilder. The hair on his chest was longer than the hair on his head.

As Max peeked out a window to make sure his date was gone, Leo said, "How many times do I have to tell you: You don't bring people over here!"

Max turned and said, "Relax, she's gone."

Leo let him have it. "That's not the point! We're supposed to be in the middle of a thing, people can't be walking around!"

Max opened the door and put a cigarette to his lips. Before he could light it, Leo interrupted him, barking, "Get your ass over here!" Max rolled his eyes and walked to the table.

This wasn't exactly the criminal enterprise I had expected.

As Max walked toward us, Leo leaned over to me and asked, "What's your name again?"

I told Leo my name was Cody. It was the first time I had ever claimed another name as my own, aside from playing the gay Mormon "Rick." But unlike my appearance in that play, I didn't know my next line.

Max joined us at the table and Leo made the introduction. "Max, this is Ronnie's friend Cody. Cody, this is my son, Max."

Max looked at me and said, "'Sup," then immediately turned to his father to say, "I need some money."

"What the hell did you do with the money I just gave you?!" Leo said.

I became invisible as father and son argued over the money Max had blown on horse races and lap dances. They didn't seem to have filters, or care what I thought. Watching them bicker, I had difficulty imagining someone as suave as Ronnie working with these bozos.

Max tried to justify his "business expenses" and his father said, "Can we talk about it later and focus on *this* now?!" Then Leo turned to me and politely offered, "Can we get you something to drink? Soda? Water?"

I declined and Leo got back to business.

"So, where did you deal with Ronnie?"

"I've never dealt with Ronnie," I said.

"Who have you dealt for?"

"I've never dealt."

Surprised, Leo said, "I'm confused. Ronnie spoke very highly of you. He said you could deal."

I was already in over my head. I explained that I *could* deal, but I was not a dealer. And although I could handle cards well and execute the moves required to cheat, I knew very little about gambling. I told Leo that I had played in a few friendly card games where the deck was passed around the table. And I used to play gin rummy with my aunt. But I had never cheated at cards, nor had I professionally dealt a game of poker in my life.

Leo was stunned. This was not what he wanted to hear. Max, on the other hand, appeared to take pleasure in seeing his father's meeting fall apart so quickly. With a smirk he said to his old man, "So I guess we're done here?"

Leo glared at Max until he dropped the stupid smirk. Then Leo turned his attention to the deck of cards on the table. He slid them toward me and said, "Shuffle those."

I gave the deck a few shuffles and cuts.

Impressed, Leo said patronizingly, "Hey, look at that! You can shuffle just fine." Then he told me, "Here we use the standard sequence: Riffle. Riffle. Box. Riffle. Cut." Which was shorthand for the shuffling procedure that casinos use: three riffle shuffles, followed by a series of cuts, then one more riffle shuffle, and one final cut onto a cut card.*

I executed the sequence like a pro. It wasn't cheating, it was just shuffling, but I was proud of myself for even knowing what the hell he was talking about.

---

* *Cut card*—a piece of plastic the same size and shape as a playing card. This card is added to the bottom of the deck after the cards are shuffled, before they are dealt. It is designed to prevent the bottom card from being flashed (shown) or dealt.

Leo started to light up; I could see a glimmer of hope in his eyes. After I completed the sequence for a second time, Leo tried to reserve his excitement, saying, "Okay. Now let's see the top card."

I turned the card on top of the deck faceup: Jack of Diamonds.

Then, as if speaking to a child, Leo instructed, "Now shuffle again, *exactly as you did before*, cuts and all, but keep the Jack on top of the deck."

Leo leaned in with anticipation. Max sat back with a smug look on his face, as if expecting me to fail the test. I could tell neither of them understood: There had only ever been one test in my life I had studied for, and this was it.

I gave the deck a few shuffles and cuts, then turned over the top card to show the Jack of Diamonds was still on top and well under my control.

"Look at that!" Leo said, excitedly tapping Max and rubbing my success in his face as if it were his own. There seemed to be a symbiotic relationship between the two men's smiles: The happier Leo was, the more Max frowned. And vice versa.

Then I could see Leo make a wish, as he asked me, "Can you second deal?"

"I think so," I said, knowing I could.

As I demonstrated second deals, Leo leaned over to Max and quietly said, "Jesus, he's as good as Ronnie."

Leo was eager to see what other stunts his new pet could do. He asked me if I could stack a hand for him.

"We play Texas hold'em[*] here. You know that game?"

I had seen *Rounders*.

"How many players?" I asked.

"Six," Leo said.

I shuffled the deck with marksman accuracy and fired off two cards each to Leo, Max, and four invisible players.

I saw Max's eyes widen as he looked at his pair of Jacks.

Then Leo yelled, "Hot damn!" and turned over his pair of Kings. He didn't even need to see the hand play out to the end. He skipped right to the hard stuff, saying, "Let's see ya cold-deck the game."

He tossed me a second deck of cards. I demonstrated how I would secretly switch one deck for another in the context of a game. Then, using false shuffles, I maintained the order of the pre-stacked deck, which I then cleanly dealt.

Leo practically leaped out of his chair with excitement while Max remained slumped with his arms folded. I couldn't understand why this guy was such a dick. I was there to save his family business, but by the way he was acting you'd think I was there to destroy it.

Looking back, I believe it was Max's less-than-sunny disposition that inspired me to ask, "Did Ronnie use the Greek deal?"[†]

---

[*] *Texas hold'em*—a form of poker in which each player is dealt two cards facedown and all players share five cards dealt faceup.

[†] *Greek deal*—a false deal that enables one to secretly deal the *second*-to-last card of the deck during play. It's a way of beating the cut card, the plastic card that is on the bottom to prevent bottom dealing.

I knew the answer was no before I asked the question. Because I knew Ronnie had never bothered to learn the Greek deal. It's a pain in the ass and, frankly, not worth the trouble. But I learned it. Because why not? And I wanted them, mostly Max, to know I could do it.

After I finished with the Greek deal, when the last card hit the table, Leo, smiling from ear to ear, said, "Kid, if you can do even half of what we've seen in a game, we're gonna be just fine." Then he turned to Max to say, "Amazing, right?"

"Yeah, it's great," Max said, forcing as close to a compliment as he'd ever give me.

Then Leo jabbed Max with "Can you believe he's younger than you?"

Max did not reply. He just stared at me. I remember thinking: *So this is what those kids who threw things at me grew up to be.*

After I passed the physical test with flying colors, Leo walked me through an average night, saying, "The donks start arriving about six o'clock—"

"Sorry," I said, cutting him off to ask, "What's a 'donk'?"

He clarified, saying, "The schmucks who come here thinking they know how to play cards."

I nodded and he continued. "They'll have some drinks, maybe some dinner, then the game starts around seven." He told me that, were I to accept the position, I was welcome to eat on the job, but I should only drink if it helped calm the nerves.

When I told Leo I didn't drink, he used that as an opportunity to bring up Max's excessive use of alcohol.

"Do I really need to be here for this?" Max asked in a huff.

Leo raised his voice ten notches to say, "You have somewhere else you gotta be?" Then he immediately caved, saying, "Nah, you can go."

"I still need money," the brat said.

Leo reached into his back pocket and produced a wad of cash the size of a softball. It appeared to consist of only hundred-dollar bills. He peeled off a chunk to create a smaller but still substantial wad of money for Max. Handing it over, Leo said, "This needs to last you a week!"

I had no idea how much money was there. I didn't want to know.

Max started to walk away, but his father, once again, stopped him and forced him to be a human being, saying, "Forgetting something?"

Max looked at me and said, "Nice to meet you."

I couldn't say the same, so I just said, "Thanks."

When Max vanished down the hall, Leo looked at me and asked, "You get along with your dad?"

"I don't have a dad," I said.

"No?" He seemed genuinely curious to hear my story. But I didn't indulge him. Instead, I asked a question that popped into my mind: "So, do the players that come here think this is just a casual game at your house?"

"Not *my* house," he said.

"Sorry, I assumed it was yours. Whose house is this?"

"I don't know."

Later I found out they were renting the place for what I can only assume was an astronomical monthly lease.

I asked, "So who do the players think lives here?"

"They don't ask," he said, matter-of-fact.

That answer floored me. "How is that possible?"

"Do you ask, 'Who owns this place?' when you go to a whore-house?"

"I've never been to a—"

He cut me off. "Cody, these guys aren't coming here to make friends. Everyone who comes here is chasing something. And knowing who owns this house ain't gonna help 'em catch it. Now where were we?"

"The players arrive at six and the game starts at seven."

"Right. So, if you want to stick to Ronnie's schedule: He started dealing around nine. He liked letting the donks get into the groove before he started busting them up."

Confused, I interrupted, "Who deals before nine?"

"The other dealers."

"Other dealers?"

A serious poker game, like the game in that house, can last for twelve, fifteen hours, even two days. It's common to have multiple dealers in rotation so the game can continue, nonstop. So, if I were to accept the gig, I'd be working alongside other *legitimate* dealers, professionals who were hired through a reputable service.

Then Leo went on to explain that, aside from the dealers, they hired a bartender to mix drinks, servers to deliver them to the guests, a chef and a kitchen staff to cook meals upon request. Sometimes they even had a masseuse come to give players back rubs at the table.

"We can't give them any reason to leave," Leo said. "It's not a tournament. These guys can get up at any time and walk away with whatever money they have left."

I had thought this game was just a few guys sitting around a card table. But it was so much bigger. It was an elaborate production designed to lure players in and keep them there until all their money was gone.

I asked Leo, "How many of the *other* employees know about the scam? How many knew Ronnie was cheating?"

"None of them," he said. "The only people who knew about Ronnie were me and Max . . . and now you."

That was the moment I got nervous. Taking this gig didn't just require me to keep and wield secrets; it required that I become one. Adding to the stress, I had assumed that cheating at cards was a selfish and irresponsible act. But accepting this job meant taking on responsibilities greater than I could have imagined. The entire economy of that house orbited around Ronnie's ability to cheat the game. If he didn't do his job well, it all came crashing down. This level of responsibility intimidated me.

I felt the walls closing in, and I hadn't even accepted the gig. Leo must have sensed I was getting overwhelmed, because he said, "But you don't need to worry about *any* of that. The only thing you'd need to worry about is dealing winning hands to me, Max, and the Honest John."

Too late. I was worrying about plenty. Including the disturbing information that Max would be sitting at the table. I didn't even enjoy sitting in the same room with him; the last thing I wanted to do was help a guy like that win.

"Do the players know you and Max are related?" I asked.

"Sure, they don't care," he said flippantly.

It seemed suspicious to me that a father and son would be at the same table, but he assured me it wasn't. He said it was common for players to bring friends or family to join the table, or just to cheer them on. Some guys brought girlfriends. He said one guy even brought his mom. Then Leo made himself chuckle, saying, "Come to think of it, the only people that they don't bring are their wives."

"Wait," I said. "Who is Honest John?"

"Honest John's not a person," he corrected me. "It's multiple people."

I stared blankly.

"Look, it'd be too obvious if Max and I were the only people who ever won in this house," he explained. "So, we have a rotation of guys who come sit and win for us. Only they don't know we're cheating."

I didn't entirely understand what he meant, so he went over it slowly and carefully. I was astounded by what he told me:

Leo paid professional poker players—guys I had seen play on TV, including two World Series of Poker champions—to sit at his table and play cards. Leo staked them to play in the game, allowing them to keep a portion of their winnings. If they lost, it was on Leo.

What Leo *didn't* tell the poker pros was that they *couldn't* lose, because Ronnie would be dealing them winning hands all night. From the pros' perspective, this was a no-brainer: They were being paid to play poker with zero financial risk. From Leo's perspective: He got professional card players to draw crowds *and* unknowingly clean his money for him.

It's hard to overstate how diabolical this ploy was. News of a poker champ sitting at a card table in a private game would spread through LA like wildfire. The players would show up, eager to go head-to-head against the guy wearing a World Series bracelet. If they won (they wouldn't), they got bragging rights for life. If they lost (they would), they got to say they sat down with a great. Best of all, the Honest Johns were oblivious to the scam, hence the name. When they won (which was always) they genuinely believed they were winning on their own merits. And if, for whatever reason, the Johns were ever compelled to tell the truth, the only thing they could admit to was being paid to play, which is frowned upon in some circles, but not against the rules.

I was so blown away by the elegance of this gambit, I almost forgot about the anxiety I had been experiencing. One thing baffled me, though. I couldn't understand how Leo compelled World Series of Poker champions to sit at his table. I understood that money is money, but why would they do that for *him*?

The answer was on Leo's right wrist. He had won a World Series of Poker tournament back in the '90s, and he had the gold bracelet to prove it. Which meant Leo, a well-respected card player, could probably beat every amateur who sat at his table playing on the square. So why cheat, then? Why risk ruining his reputation? Was it the money? What was *he* chasing?

Wrapping up our meeting, Leo said, "If you deal for us, you'll make exactly what Ronnie made: ten percent of what we take in."

I asked, "How much do you guys pull in on an average night?"

"About 100K. On a good night, 150."

The idea of making *ten thousand dollars* in one night was beyond my comprehension.

"What do you say?" Leo asked. "You in?"

I remember the meeting like it was yesterday. I can smell the fresh paint and picture Leo in that Pepto-Bismol–colored shirt. I see the green felt on the card table and can feel the cards I was handed. I can perfectly picture my awkward introduction to Max and the grimace he made for most of our encounter. I recall how pathetic he was taking money from his father, how much I envied him for being able to ask, and the solace I felt knowing I could do something that he never could.

I remember it all, including the moment Leo leaned toward me with a conspiratorial twinkle in his eye and asked, "You in?"

But I don't remember saying, "Yes."

I must have blinked, because it's as if someone stole those frames from the movie of my life. When I play back that moment, I hear him ask the question, then everything goes black and silent. When the image returns, Leo is smiling like the Cheshire cat and I'm shaking his hand.

He said, "Welcome aboard. When do you think you can be ready for a game?"

"I have no idea," I said.

"Can you be ready by Friday?" he asked.

"I'm not sure," I said. That was only five days away.

"Here's an idea," he said. "Your *hands* are ready to work today. We just need to get you up to speed on all the dealer's procedures. So, why don't we have you just start working as a regular dealer? You can deal on the square until you're comfortable. Sound good?"

I was comfortable with that. As long as I didn't have to cheat, there was nothing to be nervous about.

I told him, "Sounds like a plan."

He escorted me out. Before he opened the front door, he pulled the wad of cash from his pocket and asked, "You got a girl?"

I nodded. He peeled off five hundred bucks and handed it to me, saying, "Thank her for letting us borrow you."

Outside and down the stone steps, I waited for the gate to open. I turned back to see Leo wave goodbye. I waved back and exited the property.

I got into my car and started it. Before making the U-turn to head back down the winding road, I noticed the CHECK ENGINE light was off. I had the thought: *Perhaps it's a sign. Maybe this was meant to be.*

FIRST HAND

The moment we knowingly conceal information from others we set a boundary between ourselves and those who do not possess the knowledge. This boundary provides us with a space of privacy and privilege. It can be used to shield us from pain and protect us from harm. Or it can act as a barrier, built to exclude and oppress those deemed unworthy of access.

The moment we knowingly conceal information from others we create a boundary between ourselves and those who do do not possess the knowledge. This boundary provides us with a space of privacy and privilege. It can be used to shield us from pain and protect us from harm. Or it can act as a barrier, built to exclude and oppress those deemed unworthy of access.

I arrived around 8:00 p.m. Instead of pulling up in front of the house, I parked a quarter mile down the road. That's where "the help" parked, and we didn't want it to appear as though I was receiving special treatment.

I called Vanessa from the car to tell her I had arrived and that I'd be unavailable for a while. She wasn't thrilled. The only reason she was supporting this endeavor was because she knew how much it meant to me, what Ronnie meant to me.

Earlier that week she had expressed concern for my safety, asking, "What happens if someone catches you?"

I had been caught palming cards before, but that was during a card trick. It was embarrassing, but the only thing bruised was my ego. This was different, and the truth was there was no way of knowing what would happen if I got caught. But I also knew that wouldn't put her mind at ease.

So I told Vanessa what Ronnie once told me, after I asked the same question: "Most likely they'd yell, demand their money back, and leave. And the really bad guys will ask for their money back and then demand you let them in on the scam."

She didn't guilt me or give me a hard time. She just told me she loved me and made me promise to "be safe." I suppose she knew I couldn't afford the distraction.

After hanging up, I locked my phone and my wallet in the glove box. I wasn't comfortable carrying anything with my personal information into the house. Taking only my keys, I began my trek up the hill.

I fiddled with the keys as I marched up the incline because I didn't have anywhere to put them. The day after my audition, Leo had called and asked me for my measurements. Vanessa dug out the seamstress measuring tape, told me to hold still, and jotted down notes. I called Leo back and read him my numbers. The following day, a box arrived on my doorstep. Inside the box was my dealer's uniform: One pair of black pants. One pair of black shoes. Two identical white button-down shirts. A black name tag with the name CODY. And a note that read: *Do Not Open the Pockets.* I didn't know what that meant until I tried the pants on and found all the pockets had been sewn shut.

I called Leo and asked, "What's up with these pockets?"

"Theft prevention," he said. He explained that the dealers were required to sew their pockets shut to prevent them from purloining money and chips. And because the *other* dealers had to do it, I had to do it. At first, I appreciated the irony and found it humorous to think that the lack of pockets would prevent a determined thief. Walking up the hill, I was annoyed that I didn't have anywhere to put my car keys.

As I approached the property, I saw a line of exotic cars on the gravel in front of the vine-covered wall. It looked like a car show, each more impressive than the last. The two nicest, a Ferrari and an I-don't-know-what, were permitted to park in the driveway beyond the gate. I had never cared about cars a day in my life, but these machines demanded even my attention.

Atop the stone path, standing in front of the red door, was a bear-sized man in a designer turtleneck. He was holding a clipboard and speaking to a smaller man dressed like a lumberjack, in jeans and an orange flannel shirt. As I approached, the guy in the flannel nodded in my direction and the brute readied his clipboard.

"Name?" he asked.

I said, "Cody." The name felt like a veil of anonymity so sheer that the slightest wind could blow it away.

Then the doorman asked, "Last name?"

Nobody told me I'd need a last name. "Oh, I'm working tonight," I said.

"Everyone's on the list. If you're not on the list, I can't let you in."

I rambled: "I'm the new dealer. Leo hired me."

"Who?"

I had no idea what Leo's last name was. I never asked. The man in flannel shook his head. I wasn't even in the front door and I was already raising suspicion.

Suddenly, the red door opened and Leo appeared wearing the same pink shirt I had seen him in before, but with pants and brown loafers. He shouted, "Jesus Christ, Cody, where the hell have you been?!"

The doorman's demeanor and tone instantly changed. He said, "Sorry, Mr. C., I didn't know he was with you."

Leo told him not to worry about it, and I made my way into the house. As I passed the man in flannel, I noticed the gun and badge intentionally displayed on his hip.

Once inside, Leo closed the door and said, "Sorry, I forgot to add your name to the list. They shouldn't give you any trouble now."

"No problem," I said, then leaned in to ask, "Was that a cop?"

"Yeah, don't worry about him," Leo said.

For a couple hundred bucks, Leo got an off-duty LAPD officer to stand at the front door as a warning sign to would-be troublemakers. Like everyone else in that house, the cop thought it was just a poker game.

Clearly in a rush, Leo said, "Follow me," and he breezed through the living room with me in tow. I hardly recognized the place without the plastic tarps covering the hardwood floors and leather furniture. The poker table was nowhere in sight, and the smell of paint had been replaced with the scent of cigar smoke.

We sped past an attractive waitress who served a cocktail to a man wearing an Adidas tracksuit. We squeezed by two other men, sipping beers, with their jackets off, sleeves rolled up, ties loosened, and headed down the hall I had seen Max emerge from earlier that week. Leo was walking with purpose, a few steps ahead of me, when a slender man wearing a cowboy hat popped out of the bathroom, drying his hands on his jeans.

Leo stopped and said, "Hey, I want you to meet my sister's kid."

For a moment I thought he was introducing me to his nephew. Then I realized he was presenting *me* as his nephew.

He told the cowboy, "Cody's out here from Arizona. His mother is going through a real nasty divorce. She's a total mess. So I tell her, 'Send the boy to LA. Let me look after him while you figure out your shit.' Anyway, you'll be seeing him around."

I didn't know Cody had a backstory. This was the first I was hearing of it.

"Pleasure to meet you, Cody," the cowboy said, before moseying on his way.

As we continued down the hall, I turned to Leo and asked, "Who was that?"

Leo stopped, looked at the man as he walked away, then back at me to say, "No idea."

"Why did you tell him I was your nephew?" I was surprised he didn't think that was information I should've heard before he told a stranger.

"I had to give Eddie a reason to hire you," he said.

"Who's Eddie?" I asked.

"He's your boss."

"I thought *you* were my boss." I was growing increasingly anxious by the second.

Correcting himself: "What I mean is, Eddie *thinks* he's your boss."

Leo then explained something he *really* should have told me the day we met:

The house was the equivalent of a small nightclub, complete with kitchen and bar staff. Someone needed to keep the fridge stocked with steaks, make sure the bar had plenty of booze, and pay the crew at the end of each night.

Leo didn't want to deal with any of that, he wanted to focus on the action at the table and nothing else. So he'd hired a former wedding DJ, Eddie, to oversee the staff and handle the administrative grunt work. As Leo told it, "He gets paid to spend my money and walk around the house like a big shot."

Leo never told Eddie about Ronnie because he didn't want to pay for his silence. So Eddie had no idea that the universe in that house orbited around cheating the players. As far as Eddie was concerned, Ronnie was just "Leo's favorite dealer," who had been working there before Eddie was even hired.

Eddie had hired *everyone but* Ronnie, including the other legitimate dealers who had cycled through. When Ronnie "vanished" (Leo never revealed that Ronnie had been arrested), Eddie took it upon himself to hire another dealer from the reputable agency he had been using.

But Leo didn't need another dealer. He needed another Ronnie. And you can't find those at a reputable agency. I was as close to a replacement as Leo was going to find, even though I had never dealt a real game in my life. While I could handle cards well, it was a safe bet that I'd be a pretty awful dealer. So Leo needed to find a reason for introducing me, a totally unseasoned dealer, to the game. There was only one believable narrative that could justify replacing a competent professional with an inept amateur: nepotism.

Leo spun a tale, telling Eddie that I was his nephew. He claimed my mother (Leo's imaginary sister) was going through a divorce and that I was coming to LA for a fresh start. To help me out, Uncle Leo "asked" Eddie to give me a job dealing. He told him I had some dealing experience but still needed to be shown the ropes.

Leo told me all of this standing outside the double doors at the end of the hall. He made sure I understood the complexity of my role, speaking softly: "Whatever happens, just remember: This guy isn't your boss, he only thinks he is. So let him feel like he's in control. If there's a problem, come to me later."

I was still struggling not to obsess about the cop at the front door while trying to absorb the family backstory I had just received, and now I was being told to allow the boss I didn't know I had to continue believing he was my boss even though he wasn't? My head was spinning. I had been in the house three minutes and was beginning to think I wasn't going to make it through the night.

Before I could respond, Leo said, "You're doing great." Then he winked and opened the doors. Inside was a study, dimly lit with gorgeous built-in bookshelves, all tragically empty. In front of the shelves was a mahogany desk fit for a monarch. Seated at that desk was an oafish simpleton, Eddie, who appeared to be in his fifties. He had strangled his hair into a ponytail and his belly insisted his shirt remained untucked.

Growing up, I could never understand how my grandfather could have worked for mobsters at the hardware store for years without knowing it. Then I met Eddie.

"Eddie, this is my sister's kid, Cody," Leo said. (He always introduced me by saying, "This is my sister's kid," as if he didn't know the word "nephew.")

Eddie said, "Pleasure to meet you," and extended a cold, limp hand, which I shook.

Behind me, Leo said, "All right, Cody, you do what Eddie tells you. I'll see you at the table." By the time I turned around, he was already out the door.

I turned back to Eddie, who was leaning back in his chair with his fingers interlaced on his belly. He told me to take a seat and then he spoke bluntly, saying, "Let's get one thing straight: You're only here because of your uncle, you know that, right?"

"Yes, sir."

"I don't want you to think you're getting special privileges. I run a tight ship around here."

I told him I really appreciated the opportunity, which he seemed to believe. Then he moved to a large wooden cabinet and opened the door. Inside the cabinet was a gun safe. Eddie used his body to block the safe as he spun the combination lock. He opened it and clanked around for a moment. Then he turned around holding a tray lined with an assortment of poker chips, sorted by color into their own rows. He set the chips on the desk and pointed vaguely in their direction as he said, "Fives. Twenty-fives. One hundreds. Got it?"

I hadn't gotten it. "Sorry, could you repeat that?"

He rolled his eyes and, as if I had a learning disability, repeated it at half speed: "The red chips are five dollars. The green ones are twenty-five dollars. Blacks are one hundred. Got it now?"

Not really, but I nodded as if I did.

He explained that each dealer (on this night, myself and one other) received a tray loaded with two thousand dollars in chips at the beginning of the shift. These chips were to be used for making change and collecting the rake.[*]

"There's a rake?" I asked, surprised by yet another detail.

"How do you think we pay for all this?" he said as though I were an idiot.

He got that line from Leo. If anyone ever bitched about the rake, which happened from time to time, Leo would say, "How else are we supposed to pay for this?"

---

[*] *Rake*—the fee taken by the operators of a poker game. It is essentially a tax on the game, generally 2 to 5 percent of each pot, up to a predetermined maximum amount.

The real answer to that question was: cheating. The truth was the rake only collected a few thousand dollars a night, barely enough to cover the cost of food and booze. But the rake wasn't just implemented to mitigate the cost of doing business; it was also an alibi. If anyone ever questioned how the event was paid for, there was a clean answer: the rake.

Eddie went on to explain that I'd be working in two-hour shifts, although they could be longer. If I had to use the bathroom or leave the table for any reason, I was to tell one of the servers and they'd tell Eddie, who would send in the other dealer to relieve me.

He concluded, "At the end of the night, you come back here, I'll count you out. Capeesh?"

I nodded, overwhelmed. I needed a minute to focus, to go over everything I had just heard, and to reconcile it with what I already knew.

"It's not rocket science!" he said, already annoyed by my lack of experience. Then he grabbed a small flashlight from his desk and said, "Stand up, let's see your pockets."

The ridiculous idea of sewing the dealers' pockets shut came from Eddie. He saw it done in a casino once. It was one of those ideas you throw out there when you have nothing else to offer. Leo didn't object; he wanted Eddie to feel as if he had something to contribute. The more king-like Eddie felt, the less likely it was that he'd ever realize he was a pawn.

He came around the desk and shined the light on my pockets. After he circled me, Eddie clicked the light off and asked, "You gotta take a leak?"

I told him I was fine. He moved toward the door, saying, "All right, let's go."

"I'm going out there now?"

"Hell yeah you're going out now! My other guy needs a break and you need the practice. So let's go!"

My stomach dropped and I froze. I felt like a soldier being told it was time to go into the trenches. Eddie raised an eyebrow and stared at me expectantly. I had no idea what he wanted. Again, feeling like an actor without his next line, I just stood there, staring back, expecting him to help.

He threw me a bone, looking at the tray of chips on the desk.

"Oh, right," I said, picking them up while Eddie shook his head in dismay.

As we left the study and walked to the opposite side of the house, I kept repeating to myself: *The red chips are five dollars. The green ones are twenty-five dollars. Blacks are one hundred.*

We moved down *another* long hallway to arrive at a set of double doors with frosted-glass panels. Eddie opened the door and said, "After you."

The walls of the game room were dark blue. Two enormous flat-screen TVs competed for attention on opposing walls. Scattered throughout the room was a treasure trove of autographed sports memorabilia: a pair of Muhammad Ali's gloves, a rookie card signed by Michael Jordan, and a baseball with a faint signature that read *Mickey Mantle*. (All forgeries, of course; Leo actually went to the trouble of finding signatures on the Internet, and then, using tracing paper, transferring those phony autographs to the objects. After all, the devil is in the details.)

In the center, below the ceiling fan, was the poker table. Six players sat there drinking, solemnly checking their cards, and placing bets. Seated across from them was a Hispanic man in his mid-forties, dressed identically to me, whose name tag read: ALBERTO.

"That's Bert," Eddie said, pointing. "After he finishes this hand, go tap him on the shoulder and he'll get up."

I suddenly realized my hands were so cold I couldn't feel the chip rack I was holding. I needed my hands to work. I turned to Eddie and asked him if it was still okay if I ran to the restroom. After he begrudgingly obliged, I handed him my chip rack and ran.

I locked the door behind me and ran my hands under scalding water until I couldn't take it anymore. Then I turned the heat down and splashed some water on my face. After drying off, I gave myself a pep talk, reminding myself that all I had to do was deal a few hands of poker. No cheating. Just shuffling, dealing, and moving some chips around the table.

I returned to the game room with bright red hands. By the time I took the tray back from Eddie, I could feel the icicles re-forming.

"Did you piss yourself?" Eddie asked with a look of disgust.

I looked down to see my pants were soaked from leaning against the sink. Not off to a great start.

"It doesn't matter, get in there." He all but shoved me toward the game.

I arrived at the table and stood behind Bert, who gathered up the cards and addressed the players, saying, "Well, that's it for me tonight, gentlemen. It's been a pleasure!" He waited a beat for the players to toss him a tip. They didn't even look at him.

"Okay. Good luck, gentlemen."

Bert removed his chip tray from the table, stood up, and turned to me, asking, "You the new guy?"

"I am."

Bert smiled, saying, "Welcome, brother!" Then he leaned in to say, "Don't expect any tokes* from these cheap bastards." He gave me a chummy pat on the back and left.

I had only known him all of three seconds and I already missed him.

I placed my tray into the open table cavity and sat down across from the players. Directly to my left was Leo. To my right, I recognized the cowboy I had met in the hall. The four players between them were blurry, unfamiliar faces.

It took everything I had to say my first line: "Good evening, gentlemen."

Leo, the only friendly face, said, "Hello, dealer," and took a puff of his cigar. The others barely acknowledged my existence. They just wanted their next hand.

I fought through the frost in my fingers and began to shuffle the cards Bert had left behind. Eddie hovered in the background, watching me. Leo must have read my mind because I saw him lean back and shoo Eddie away.

I finished the shuffles, completed the cut onto the cut card, and began to deal. Two cards in and a player said, "What the

* *Tokes*—slang for "tips."

hell, dealer!?" The gruff fellow who spoke up appeared bewildered and annoyed. I scanned the table and spotted my mistake. *He* was supposed to be the first player, but I had skipped him entirely.

In other words, I fucked up on the very first card of my very first hand. I reminded myself to breathe and figured no harm, no foul, since I had dealt only two cards and nobody had looked at them. *Why not just move them to the correct seats?* I thought, reaching across the table to slide the two cards to their proper recipients. The table grumbled with displeasure.

Leo said, "It's a misdeal." I must have appeared confused because he added, "You gotta start over."

So I reshuffled and cut the cards, then dealt, starting with the first unhappy customer.

I finished dealing the players their hole cards[*] and one of them frustratedly said, "Come on, dealer, what are you waiting for?!" Again, I scanned to see what I had missed, but they each had two cards and everything looked as it should. I sat there confused until Leo again helped, saying, "The flop, dealer."

In card games in the movies, when players fold, they do it with flair and say, "I'm out," or "Too rich for my blood!" When they bet, they say things like "I bet one hundred," and then the

---

[*] *Hole cards*—cards that players must keep secret (their identities hidden) from the rest of the table. Almost all modern poker variants make use of hole cards. In Texas hold'em, players are each dealt two hole cards on the first betting round, which they use in conjunction with community cards to make a hand.

next guy says, "Let's make it five hundred." They do this back and forth until someone says, "Call."

That's what I was expecting. Instead, nobody said a word. They just gently pushed the chips a few inches in front of them, or silently slid their cards toward the center, or lightly tapped the table. Without saying a word, everyone seemed to know exactly what was happening at all times, every step of the way. Except for me.

Everyone at that table had already placed their bets or folded for that round, and I didn't even notice. They would have kept moving on without me, but they needed me to deal the next three cards. When I looked up, I thought I was still with them, but that's only because they had already lapped me.

The most stressful moment was at the conclusion of the hand. As the dealer, it was my job to look at the cards on the table, determine who'd won, and push the chips to the victor. After the players revealed their hands, if I didn't push the chips toward the winner within five seconds, one of the players would yell at me. Sometimes it was the winner, eager to sort his riches, who'd yell, "Come on, dealer!" Other times, it was the loser who'd take his recent sting out on me with a rude "Let's go!" Either way, it was never about the money. It was always about getting to the next hand. Before anyone could move on, the winner had to be paid. And to do that, the dealer had to determine the winner. That determination is made by reading the hands.

Generally speaking, players learn to read hands naturally and quickly over the course of thousands of hands. Dealers must learn the skill and hone it; they practice and run drills to ensure they are faster at absorbing the hands than any player at the table. (It's literally their job to be faster.) The dealer must not only read the hands instantly, but accurately. As a dealer, the *last* thing you want to do is push the money toward the wrong player.

Forty minutes into dealing, I misread the hands and pushed the winnings toward the *loser*. The table erupted. The guy who *actually* won was so furious he demanded they bring Bert, the other dealer, back. The others seemed more than agreeable to the idea.

So much for learning on the job.

To be honest, it was so brutal and I was so mentally taxed and disoriented, I welcomed their rejection. Had they proposed a flogging, I might have preferred that to dealing another hand. I knew it was bad when I was happy to see Eddie, who had entered the room and was practically running toward the table.

Leo stopped him in his tracks and silenced the table, saying, "He's green, for Chrissake! Let him deal and he'll figure it out!"

The whole table grumbled, knowing they were stuck with me. It was "Uncle" Leo's game, and as long as he wanted me there, I wasn't moving. No one was more disappointed than I. Nepotism wasn't as great as I thought it'd be.

The second hour was better than the first, but still awful. I continued making every mistake imaginable: I forgot to burn a card before a turn. I accidentally gave someone the wrong amount of change, overpaying him, but thankfully the recipient

acknowledged my mistake. I forgot to move the dealer button*
so frequently, the table just started doing it for me. I misjudged
a stack of chips and announced the wrong amount for a raise, the
irony being that the players already knew how much was being
wagered because they, unlike me, could look at a stack of chips
and tell the difference between $525 and $575.

By the time Bert returned to give me a break, the players
didn't just want me off the table, they wanted me dead. And I
hadn't even cheated.

"Way to hang in there," Bert encouraged me.

I muttered, "Thanks," and stumbled out of the room. Seeing
Bert holding his chip tray was the only reason I remembered to
take mine with me when I left.

Eddie was waiting for me in the hall. He said, "You've got a
lot to learn."

I wanted to say, "No shit," but I just said, "I know."

He told me to go back into the room and watch Bert deal, to
"absorb a thing or two."

Like a good soldier, I returned, sat in the corner, and watched
Bert deal from a safe distance. He was, of course, an excellent
dealer and made it all look effortless. But I didn't have the energy
to focus on him. My whole body was sore and my brain felt like
mush.

---

* *Dealer button*—a round disk that indicates the position of the first card to
be dealt. The dealer button rotates clockwise after each hand, just as the deal
would rotate under standard poker rules.

The next thing I knew, Eddie was telling me to get some dinner. I didn't realize how hungry I was until I caught a whiff of garlic as I approached the kitchen. I introduced myself to the chef and requested a filet.

The chef replied, "Sorry, the steaks are reserved for the players."

He handed me a paper plate with a mound of penne pasta, a stick of garlic bread, and a side salad with more carrots than lettuce.

I sat outside by the shimmering pool, feeling defeated, dreading the thought of returning to the table. I remember thinking I should just get up, walk out the front door, and never look back. But I didn't. Instead, I just stared into the hypnotic blue water and ate my cold pasta.

Eventually, Eddie came outside and said, "I've been looking all over for you. Time to go back in."

I stood up like a battered fighter who had just heard the bell, going back for round two.

Eddie walked behind me down the hall, as if escorting me to the gallows. If it were up to him, I would never be allowed to sit at that table again. As far as Eddie was concerned, he was in charge of running the game and I was making him look bad. Which is true, I was. But Leo insisted I get the flight time.

"After this you can go home," he said. "Bert said he can handle the rest of the night on his own."

Thank god for Bert.

It was midnight and I was grateful to see only four players remained at the table: Leo, the cowboy, and two others. I was especially thankful to see that the guy who'd demanded my removal was gone. When I stood behind Bert to tap him out, the players groaned, lamenting my return, knowing whatever fun they were having was about to come to a screeching halt.

"Good evening again, gentlemen," I said to the unhappy bunch.

What's strange is that I genuinely wanted to do a good job as a dealer and actually felt bad for subjecting the players to my incompetence. I felt the sharp sting of exasperated breaths and disapproving looks. It was the same feeling I had when I (briefly) waited tables. I felt guilty every time a customer's food was wrong, or when they had to remind me to bring something they had already asked for, or when I accidentally spilled their drinks. When they didn't tip me, I didn't get angry; I thought, *I must not have done a good job*. I wanted to be a good dealer, not just so I could eventually cheat them, but because I didn't want them to suffer.

I decided to adjust my approach. I had pinned down the two areas that were giving me the most trouble—keeping up with the action and reading the hands—and formulated a work-around: Before each hand began, I forced myself to move the dealer button. Then I shuffled, cut, and dealt, making sure to start at the correct position. After that, I reminded myself to collect the rake, then I stopped focusing on the procedures. Instead, I turned my attention to the players.

I wasn't fast enough to lead the action around the table. But I was *almost* fast enough to follow it. I watched their hands as they tapped the table, or tossed the cards, or pushed chips forward, but I didn't bother trying to call out amounts for bets. I also knew that it was impossible for me to read the hands as quickly as the players did. So, when it came time to determine the winner, instead of looking at the cards on the table, I looked up to see their reactions. Their faces instantly revealed more than the cards. It wasn't a science, but it was a safe bet to push the money toward the happiest player.

Over the next two hours, I still made plenty of errors, but none of them got me yelled at. It was a vast improvement over my first round, and I considered this second shift a minor victory.

At some point, Bert relieved me of my duties, telling me, "Great job tonight," saying it as if he meant it. Considering how the night had begun, I was pleased to go out on a good note.

I walked to the study where I'd first met Eddie. The house was quieter than before. The chef was cleaning the stove. The bartender had gone home, and the server was reading a book at the bar.

Eddie was seated at his desk. I placed my tray on the desktop and sat across from him as he counted the chips. Suddenly there was a knock and I heard Leo say, "Cody?"

When he saw I was cashing in for the night, he entered the room and said, "Whoa, where are you going?"

Eddie spoke for me: "He's done for the night."

"Like hell he is! He's doing great out there," Leo said.

"Bert has got it covered for the rest of the night."

Puffing up his chest, Leo said, "Bullshit! He's going back in tonight." He looked at me, sternly said, "Keep up the good work," then stormed out.

Eddie shook his head and pushed my chip tray toward me without saying a word. I assumed he was angry about being undermined. But what was clear was that Eddie was confused; he couldn't comprehend why Leo would want to subject the players, or even himself, to more of my ineptitude. I watched him struggle from the other side of the secret.

I was ready to go home, exhausted and mentally battered. But it was not to be. I exited the study and was intercepted by Leo in the living room. He was standing at the glass doors that led out back. He waved me over and I joined him on the patio as he chomped and puffed on his cigar.

"How you feeling?" he asked.

I told him, "The first round was rough, but I think I'm getting the hang of it."

"Well, you're doing great. Sorry if Eddie is giving you a hard time."

I told him Eddie was fine.

Then Leo blew out a big puff of smoke before saying, "Listen, the next time you sit down, I want you to cold-deck the game."

I stared at him in amazement. And horror. "I thought you said tonight was dealing on the square, to get the hang of it."

"Yeah, I thought so, too. But then I saw how great you're doing."

"Are you kidding? I'm not ready. Did you see me out there? Those guys already want my head on a pike."

"I saw you. You looked like a rookie dealer. And that's *exactly* why you need to get back in there and cold-deck the sons-a-bitches."

When I remained speechless, Leo said, "You're right, those guys think you are a terrible dealer. In fact, they think you are the *worst* dealer they've ever seen. Which means, never in a *million years* could any of them fathom you're capable of cold-decking their game. Don't you get it? Those guys think you can't even deal a straight game, there's no way in hell they're gonna think you can cheat 'em!"

It wasn't exactly the pep talk I was hoping for. In theory I understood how my weak performance as a dealer could actually *help* disguise my ability to cheat. But it didn't change the fact that I was now required to do yet another (secret) task on top of the work I was already failing to do well.

I told him I didn't think I could do it.

"Hey, I'm not gonna force you. You take all the time you need. But just in case you change your mind . . ."

He told me where to find the prearranged deck he wanted me to switch in: the trash can in the bathroom, underneath the garbage bag. And he suggested, "Bring it with you. If you don't feel comfortable, don't do it. Easy."

Easy for him to say "easy." All he had to do was sit there and look at the cards I dealt. But I wanted to seem like a team player, so I said, "Sure," and went to the bathroom to get the cards, certain I wouldn't actually use them.

In the trash can, below the plastic bag, I found the red-backed deck, identical to the cards being used in the game. I looked at the order, and from the positions of the cards I could see it was arranged for Leo to win with three Jacks. I went to place the cards into my pocket, only to be reminded that I didn't *have* any pockets. Clearly Leo hadn't thought this through. I went to return the deck to the trash can, but didn't for some reason. Instead I tucked the deck into my sock, thinking at least I could tell Leo that I'd tried.

When I returned to the room, the first thing I noticed was that the cowboy had disappeared. The game was down to three players: Leo, who was sitting upright, chomping on his cigar, and two players who slouched and looked almost as miserable as I felt.

Bert stood, in preparation for my arrival. As he picked up his chip tray, the dealer who moved with lightning precision suddenly appeared to be moving in slow motion, so slowly he was almost standing still. On the big TV screen, the basketball slowly arced toward the rim, and the player who shot it was floating in midair. Leo's cigar smoke moved like an ethereal sculpture, floating toward the ceiling fan that appeared to be spinning at a rate of one rotation every hundred years.

As I took my first step toward the table, a realization struck me so clearly that time stood still: Logistically, thinking in terms of deception, if I had wanted to switch decks I'd need to have the cards readily available, which meant removing them from my sock. I knew that once I was seated, it would be difficult to reach them without some sort of suspicious activity. The most ideal moment (perhaps the only moment) to retrieve them was the moment I sat down.

I took the eternity of that walk to make my decision. The moment I reached the table, real time resumed. I placed the chip tray in its slot and waited a beat for Bert to start to walk away. Before I sat down, I hiked my pants to expose my socks. As soon as I sat, I kicked my left foot back, pushing my heel toward the sky, high enough so my left hand could reach it. Then, under the guise of adjusting my seat, I grabbed the deck protruding from my sock and tucked it behind my left knee, where I locked it into place, should I need it later.

I didn't say "good evening" or bother with any niceties. I just grabbed the cards on the table and started shuffling. And that was the moment I knew I had reached a critical point in my journey. I had arrived at "the line."

Of course, I had heard about the line and how others managed to cross it. But I had never been close enough to it to realize it's not a line. It's a ledge. When Ronnie called, it appeared in the distance, like a horizon. I began moving toward it when I agreed to meet Leo. The next thing I knew, I was sitting at a table with a deck of cards behind my knee, staring into an abyss.

I had convinced myself to make the pilgrimage by giving myself outs along the way: I was able to tell Ronnie I would take the meeting because I knew I could say no to his boss, Leo. I accepted the job from Leo because I knew I could start as a dealer and didn't have to cheat. I only took the cards from the bathroom because I knew I wouldn't have to use them. And I took them out of my sock and wedged them behind my knee only because I knew I didn't have to switch them in.

But I had reached the very tip of the last branch on this particular decision tree. There was no moving forward or sidestepping. I had two choices: go back from whence I came, or leap into the void ahead.

I knew the world that was behind me. I found it to be unwelcoming, often unkind, and there seemed to be little use for me there. However, as dreary and taxing as that world was to me, it wasn't as terrifying as the abyss at that table. I wasn't able to commit to making the leap on my own. So, like a celestial flip of a coin, I chose to let the universe decide for me. If an opportunity were to present itself, I'd jump into the unknown. Otherwise, at the end of the game, I'd return the cards to the trash where I found them and go home.

Leo was wide-awake and focused, while the two other players fiddled with their chips and fidgeted in their seats. They were tired, but their eyes were still open and facing my direction. All talking had ceased. The only sounds in the room were the clicking of chips and the occasional shuffles. My hands were so cold they hurt. All I wanted to do was cup my mitts over my mouth and breathe to warm them up, but I thought it best I not draw attention.

At 4:00 a.m., I thought I might have missed my chance. One of the drowsy players hollered for the server. When she entered, he turned and ordered coffee. Leo was looking at me, and his eyes were pleading for me to ring in the cooler. But the third player was facing forward, waiting patiently for the game to resume. He wasn't looking at me or my hands, just staring ahead into space.

If it were a demonstration or perhaps even a performance, I would have been more than willing to trust my abilities to execute the sleight. But there were stakes now, and that made all the difference. Unwilling to risk it, I committed to the arrangement I had made with the universe and continued to deal on the square.

When the waitress returned, she set the coffee down next to the player, who reached for it unaware that the waitress's hand was returning to the same spot with a tiny cup of cream. Their hands collided and the liquid spilled onto the table and into the player's lap. It was then, when all eyes were drawn toward the chaos, the universe shoved me into the abyss.

I don't remember taking the leap, nor do I recall being airborne. It's yet another missing frame in the movie of my life. I only remember landing on the other side. I knew the deed was done when I saw a deck on the table and felt a deck now tucked behind my *right* knee.

The waitress was still apologizing and the table was distracted by the aftermath of the collision. With the hardest part behind me, I pressed on into the new unknown, simulating shuffles and creating the illusion of cuts. Then I waited for them to turn their attention back to the game. I needed to make sure they felt like they had seen the final cut. Once I was sure the table was ready to continue, I sailed the cards to each player.

I watched Leo's face when he looked at his hand. When his eyes widened, I knew even he had missed the deck switch. When the other two players looked at their cards, just as they had every time before, I understood I was nearly home free.

Leo knew he had them beat, so he made sure not to overplay his hand. He lured the two men into the trap, through the flop. He lost one of them, who folded at the turn. But he strung the other along, taking him all the way down the river, where the sucker eventually took the bait, saying, "All in."

Leo pushed his chips in, too, saying, "I know I shouldn't but what the hell."

When Leo rolled over his hand, the loser said, "Fuck! I thought I had you."

Feigning surprise, Leo said, "So did I." He won over twenty thousand dollars on that hand.

The loser quietly got up and left the table. No anger or accusations; he just got up and left. The *other* player looked at the mountain of chips in front of Leo and said, "I think that's it for me, too." Leo tried to convince him to stay, but the man insisted on leaving with what little money and dignity he had left.

After the two strangers departed, Leo turned to me and said, "What'd I tell ya."

Numb, I said, "Congratulations, sir."

Disposing of the evidence, I calmly removed the deck from behind my knee and tucked it into my sock. Then I picked up my chip tray and floated to Eddie's office.

After he counted my chips, to my surprise, Eddie handed me three hundred bucks. I was expecting to be paid by Leo, but I had forgotten that I *also* got paid as a regular dealer.

Eddie halfheartedly said, "Good job tonight. Practice. See you next week."

I thanked him and left his office. Rather than going out the front door, I quietly snuck up the stairs. Leo had told me to hide in an empty bedroom and wait for everyone else to go home. After thirty minutes he hollered, "Coast is clear!"

I came downstairs, completely exhausted. Leo was waiting for me in the living room, standing tall and proud with a huge grin. "There's the man of the hour," he said, beaming.

As I reached the bottom step, he extended his arms and pulled me in for a celebratory hug, patting me on the back. He seemed genuinely impressed, possibly even proud, I wasn't sure. Either way, he was in a better mood than I was.

"I didn't think I'd have much for you tonight, but with that last stunt you pulled, we made out all right," he said, handing me $2,500 in hundred-dollar bills.

"Do you have a bag or something I can put this in?" I asked, remembering I had no pockets.

Leo went to the kitchen, returned with a grocery bag, and sent me on my way, saying, "See you next week."

As I walked down the hill, the night's events didn't seem real. I had always believed I was technically capable of doing what I just did, but I never knew if I actually had the stones to pull it off. Were it up to me, I would have worked as a legitimate dealer for months, possibly years, before I ever attempted to cold-deck a game. But with some pressure from Leo, and a little help from the universe, I did it on my very first night. I realized I could have dealt on the square for one hundred years and still not have been ready.

I had anticipated having strong feelings of guilt or remorse after cheating at cards. But I didn't. Not for one second did I wrestle with guilt or feel the urge to give the money back. I knew it wasn't an honest living, but it felt like I had earned it.

THE GOOD SON

At a press conference, a reporter once asked Mike Tyson, "Your opponent claims to have a plan to beat you, does that concern you at all?"

Tyson replied, "Everybody has a plan until they get punched in the face."

I always liked that quote. But I didn't *really* understand it until I cheated at cards.

"Here's the plan," Leo said on the phone, preparing me for my second night of dealing. "We'll build up my bankroll early in the evening. Then Max will show up later, I'll dump my chips* to him, and you start sending hands his way."

Based on the one encounter I'd had with Max, I wasn't thrilled about the idea of dealing winning hands to him. But I didn't have much choice in the matter. There was a system and I was the new guy.

The following day, the sun was balancing on the horizon as I parked my car. I arrived before the game started, giving myself time to settle in before I had to sit at the table. I also remembered to bring a jacket so I had a place to put my keys and money at the end of the night. The doorman recognized me and let me in with a smile. As I passed by the cop, he nodded. I was feeling good. But the moment I entered through the door my hands turned to ice, the same chill I had felt before at the table.

In the living room, seated on the couch, three men enjoyed beers with their jackets off and sleeves rolled up; Leo later told me they were talent agents from a big prestigious agency. Blocking the entrance to the kitchen, two men who looked like they belonged at a biker bar were impatiently waiting for their steaks. On the chair in the corner sat a beady-eyed man who sipped a bourbon while sizing up his opponents.

I checked in with Eddie, who was preoccupied with counting chips. He seemed annoyed that I was early for my shift.

"Where do you want me to wait?" I asked.

---

* *Chip dumping*—the act of intentionally losing money to another player at the table. The overriding intention is to facilitate an illegal money transfer.

"Somewhere I can find you. Now piss off," he said.

To avoid the cluster of people in the house, I sat on the patio by the pool. But the beady-eyed man stepped outside as well, and after a moment of looking around he asked, "How you doing tonight?"

That innocent question felt like an interrogative shove, intended to knock me off-balance. He didn't mean it that way; it's just how questions felt in that house. A casual conversation was a field full of land mines. Lying felt equally dangerous as telling the truth, because I never knew what Leo had already told them.

Even speaking to the friendly staff made me uncomfortable. Every interaction felt like a performance because I wasn't myself; I was literally claiming to be someone I wasn't, there under false pretenses. They were decent folks trying to earn a living, and talking to them reminded me that I wasn't.

I was relieved when the game started and all the players filed into the blue room. I sat in the living room, blowing on my hands, trying to warm my fingers. When that didn't work, I went to the kitchen and got a cup of hot tea just to hold it.

Eddie came out and handed me my tray of chips. "You're up."

Seated where I expected to see Bert dealing was a Chinese woman wearing horn-rimmed glasses and a name tag that read KOKO. She dealt with precision; her hands were lightning-quick. I was mesmerized by the way she stacked chips; messy piles were instantly sculpted into towers.

I tried to introduce myself, expecting the friendly greeting Bert had given me. Instead she coldly said, "Hey," and left. It was the most she said to me all night.

Leo was in his favorite seat, to my left. I was surprised to see him in a floral-patterned shirt; I had grown accustomed to the pink. Moving left to right, the next three players were the talent agents, followed by an empty seat in front of me, then the two bikers, and finally the beady-eyed man.

"Hey, Cody! How you doing tonight?" Leo asked, chomping on his cigar. He was a natural showman.

I said, "I'm doing fine, sir," as I began to shuffle the cards.

Leo looked happy. He was feeding off the energy of the agents, who seemed to be having a ball, drinking and laughing. In contrast, the bikers were seriously focused as the beady-eyed man tried (and failed) to start up a conversation with them.

After the final cut of the cards, I said, "Good luck," and dealt my first hand of the night.

The previous week I had cold-decked the game once, at 4:00 a.m., for two sleepy players while they were focused on a spilled drink. While that was cheating, it hardly made me a cheater. Bust-out dealers need to be able to move many times a night, regardless of how many people are at the table or what they are focused on. Which meant I couldn't sit around waiting for the universe to spill coffee every time I needed to cheat.

I was facing a peculiar catch-22: Cheating under watchful eyes requires confidence. But the only way to gain that confidence is to cheat under watchful eyes.

So I took a page from my own playbook and started practicing in plain sight, executing moves at the table, but only when it *didn't* matter, in the offbeat moments. I dealt seconds when I burned cards. I'd throw *one* false shuffle between two legitimate shuffles. I'd palm cards right before I scrambled* the deck. In effect, I was cheating without cheating, because I perpetrated the maneuvers only at nonessential moments, without any intention of affecting the outcome of the game.

All the while, my hands were freezing. They felt like I had been storing them in a meat locker. Glances in my direction intensified the chill. Their pointy eyes felt like pinpricks on my hands as I shuffled and dealt. I had to suppress the unintentional tugging and pulling as my body attempted to retreat without my permission.

I was experiencing the intoxicating effects of the secrecy, similar to when the teacher had looked at me as I was secretly palming cards in class, or when I was sneaking a red ball under the cups at the magic shop. But those were mild forms of inebriation that unintentionally and subtly modified motor functions and speech. At the card table, the toxic effects were physically crippling and damn near psychotropic.

It's not that the techniques were any harder at the table. I could perform false shuffles and second deals in my sleep. But the context changed their potency. Sort of like having alcohol with a meal versus drinking on an airplane on an empty stomach. The stakes were so high at the table, the toxic effects of secrecy were overwhelming.

---

* *Scramble* (or *wash*)—a form of shuffling in which the cards are placed face-down, scattered, and mixed in a chaotic manner, then reassembled.

My paranoia was at an all-time high. I found myself silently narrating the experience as if I were Hunter S. Thompson. *Fucking ape won't stop staring at my hands. Look away, goddammit. And what about this weasel over here? Sneaky bastard, I see you looking. Oh god, did he see that second deal? Shut up and focus, dummy.*

I imagined how the players would react had they discovered they were being fleeced. Violent short films played out in my mind. I even had thoughts of surrender: *What if I just told them? Would they even believe me?*

I cheated without cheating for the first hour that night. With every move the players missed I gained a kernel of confidence. I began to trust the ignorance of their eyes. Slowly but surely, I started arranging winning hands for Leo and sending chips his way.

To my surprise, even though half the table had lost half their money, the mood in the room was quite festive. The agents were still having a good time and Leo was right there with them, cracking jokes and asking them questions about their famous clients. Even the bikers had loosened up. Smiles all around.

Koko returned. I left the table feeling rattled and depleted, but accomplished. I ate dinner on the patio by the pool. Halfway through my plate of pasta, Eddie popped out and said, "Leo wants you back in there."

"It's eleven thirty," I said, thinking I still had thirty minutes.

"You think I don't know that? He wants you in now. Hurry up."

I shoveled a few more bites and hustled back to the game. The moment I entered the room, I felt the tone had shifted. An obnoxious voice hassled Koko: "That was some bullshit, dealer.

You keep giving me hands like that and I'm gonna think you don't like me."

Who the fuck is the asshole?

Koko took it in stride; she had clearly dealt with assholes far worse. As I circled around the table, I recognized the heckler, seated between the agents and the bikers: It was Max. He was fully clothed, so it took me a moment to recognize him. It was eighty degrees, but he sported a thick black leather jacket, with dark sunglasses and a baseball cap.

As Koko left the table, Max continued heckling her the way a schoolboy torments his crush. When she exited, he turned his attention to me.

"Well, well, if it isn't Cody!" he said.

I said, "Hello, everyone," addressing the entire table.

Leo chewed on a toothpick with a sour look on his face. The pile of chips in front of him was half of what it was before I'd left. He had already dumped to Max, and I couldn't tell if he was actually upset or just putting on a show for the table.

I shuffled and dealt, no funny business. The first hand was always dealt on the square. It wasn't just a ritual; it was necessary to warm up. I don't recall who won. But I vividly remember, as I was preparing for the next hand, Max whined, "Jesus, dealer, hurry up."

We're on the same team, why the hell is he giving me a hard time? It was the sort of thing I expected from a stranger, but not a confederate. I brushed it off as a "character choice." It was a portent of worse things to come.

When I'd met Max, I thought he was an entitled—for lack of

a better term—piece of shit. I hadn't realized that was him on his *best* behavior. The table revealed who he really was: a goddamn monster.

It's difficult to isolate any single event that conveys the enormity of his douchebaggedness. It was more of a general and constant awfulness, as if his sole purpose was to pay tribute to himself while tearing others down.

I've heard stories about method actors terrorizing movie sets by staying in character 24/7. Apparently Jim Carrey made Miloš Forman's life hell when he refused to break character as Andy Kaufman. Daniel Day-Lewis made the crew carry him around and spoon-feed him when he played a guy with cerebral palsy. Working with Max was similar, except not only were his antics exhausting to be around, he could have gotten me killed.

Max pushed players to the limits of their patience, talking trash as he took their money. Sometimes he would aim his mouth at the wrong guy and be forced to drop the tough-guy act. Like all bullies, he was a coward. He'd see that he had pushed too far and try to deescalate the situation. He'd tell the angry opponent to calm down or claim he was just joking. But it was usually two sentences too late. When it looked like Max was about to get the lesson he so badly needed, his daddy would swoop in to save him.

Watching Leo calm the other players down was a master class in manipulation. He had a way of pinpointing what people wanted and knowing exactly what to say to placate them. At the table, the only thing the players wanted more than to beat the hell out of his son was to keep playing cards.

Funny thing, though. To me it was clear that Leo was never actually protecting his son. He was protecting what *really* mattered to him: the money. Most of the time Leo sided with Max's victims; he had a "kill him *after* the game" approach to mediation.

It was no secret Leo and Max were father and son. It would have been impossible to *not* know. When Max wasn't tormenting me or the players, he was bickering with his father. They argued like it was their own dysfunctional family dinner table. Leo would grow weary of Max running his mouth and tell his kid to "shut up and play." Instead of heeding his father's words, Max would come back with something like "Mind your own business, old man," and things escalated from there.

Leo wasn't innocent, though. Aside from having raised the despicable man-child, he got a kick out of taunting Max and seemed to enjoy humiliating him. Especially in front of others. Max would reach for a stack of chips to make a bet and Leo would taunt him with "You sure you wanna do that?" It was an unnecessary provocation that would inevitably lead to a flurry of insults hurled back and forth. Occasionally, other players would intervene. It was debilitating.

I learned to use these spats to my advantage. Their squabbles provided plenty of shade for me to cull cards or switch decks. They also helped maintain the integrity of the overall deception. To see them argue, you'd never in a million years think they'd be capable of working together—although it was hardly work for them; all they had to do was sit there and play the hands I dealt them.

The fact that I was the only reason Max *ever* won made it

especially infuriating when he aimed his mouth at me. He'd berate me and tell me to hurry up. He'd interrupt me as I was performing some sort of mental arithmetic or executing invisible gymnastics. The worst moments were when he got meta with his admonishments. These were the scariest moments.

One time, another player won and Max said, "Hey, dealer, I thought you were only supposed to deal *me* the great hands."

My hands were instantly hypothermic. *Was he trying to get me killed?* I looked at the other players, expecting one of them to react, but it was as if they hadn't heard him at all. They just fiddled with their chips and looked at their cards. Max had been saying similar things to the other dealer, so the comment didn't faze them.

On another occasion, he leaned in as I was shuffling, stared at my hands, then said, "You're not cheating, are you?"

Thankfully, I was *just* shuffling at that particular moment, which was the only reason I was able to laugh it off. But inside I was dying. I could tell by the smug look on his little rat face he thought he was so fucking clever. He got off on saying the quiet parts out loud. He knew the other players would dismiss his truth as trash talk, but it made my cortisol shoot through the roof. I began to think that's why he did it.

I had to say something to him. After a game, long after the guests and staff were gone, I caught Max in the living room and said, "Do you think you can lighten up on me out there? I've got a lot on my mind and it'd be helpful if you eased up."

He replied, "I treat you the same as I treat all the dealers. If

I'm nice to you they'll know something's up." To be fair, he had a point; Max treated all the dealers like shit.

I tried to reason with him, explaining how difficult my job was and how I already had tough challenges to overcome. But he wouldn't commit to backing off, instead continuing to justify his actions, claiming, "It makes it more believable."

The following week, Max continued to be Max. So I waited until he was out of sight and voiced my frustrations to Leo. "Can you get him to lighten up on me out there?" I asked.

He said, "Absolutely!" Then he yelled, "MAX! Get your ass in here!"

Not exactly what I had in mind.

Max came in holding a sandwich. Leo proceeded to relay the message right in front of me, saying, "Quit giving Cody a hard time out there!"

Max didn't even look at me. Instead of offering apologies, he clapped back with the same response he had given me: "You want me to give him special treatment?"

The two proceeded to argue as if I weren't there. I was astonished that at no point did it occur to either of them that the solution might be for Max to be kinder to *everyone*. But Max was never going to be kind to anyone, especially not to me.

Leo treated me with respect and appreciation because I could do things Max never could. But I gradually realized it was more than that. I was the son Leo wished he had, and he treated me as such. When I made mistakes, Leo said things like "Don't beat yourself up" and "You'll get 'em next time." Then he'd turn around and call Max an "idiot" and an "embarrassment." When Leo realized I had never been to a horse race, he spouted, "You've never played the ponies?!" Then I saw the disgust and jealousy on Max's face when Leo eagerly exclaimed, "That's it, I'm taking you to the track this week!"

Max softened his hazing at the table. But he started doing something even more malicious. He began intentionally losing money. I'd spend an evening building up his bankroll only to see Max piss it away on a hand I didn't rig for him. I could never prove he was doing it intentionally, but I was certain of it. He was doing it to spite me, to drag me down with him.

One night, after letting some donk walk away with our hard-earned cash, Leo yelled and screamed at his son. Max defended himself, claiming, "It's poker! Shit happens." The fact that Max was a reckless moron long before I came around was his best defense. Leo ended the spat by raising his voice and telling Max, "It's not poker! It's a job any idiot can do. Or so I thought! Just sit there and play the hand Cody gives you." Leo landed the final blow, saying, "Get it through your thick skull: I don't need you," then pointing at me to say, "I need him."

CONS AND PROS

|

"Did you speak to Ronnie?" Leo asked, handing me a stack of cash.

"No, is he okay?"

"Yeah, he's getting out in a couple weeks."

What? How? It feels like I just started.

Five months had flown by.

I was thrilled that Ronnie was getting out and felt a sense of accomplishment knowing I had kept the operation running for him. But, surprisingly, I was also disappointed that my time in that house was coming to an end. The attachment had snuck up on me.

After several months and dozens of games, I had become a serviceable dealer. Not as fast as Koko or as precise as Bert, but

I was decent. Especially when you consider that I was also dou-
bling as a cheat.

While I probably couldn't have admitted it at that time, I was
beginning to enjoy playing the part of Cody. When I'd began, I
hated presenting myself as someone I wasn't. It stressed me out
as much, even more at times, than cheating did.

Cody was an uncomfortable mask I couldn't wait to take off.
Away from the table, I avoided talking to both the players and
the staff, out of fear of being exposed. I hid in the corners of the
house reading books on my breaks; I avoided eye contact and
small talk.

Of course, that's exactly what I did when I *wasn't* Cody. I had
been hiding in corners and in the backs of rooms since I was a
boy. I learned to keep secrets to protect my family, to protect
myself, but I took it to the extreme. The word "secret" comes
from the Latin *secretus*, which means "to separate" or "set apart,"
and that's what I became: a boy set apart from the world.

But Cody had no reason to hide. As far as anyone in that
house was concerned, he was just another dealer. I was the only
thing preventing Cody from being real. As Walt would've said, I
was running when nobody was chasing me.

At some point, I stopped thinking of Cody as *other*. It wasn't
a conscious shift. I realized that it had occurred the night Bert
casually asked Cody, "How's your mother doing?" and, without
hesitation or thought, I honestly replied, "She's doing well."

It was an extraordinary moment of mundanity. When Bert
had asked me (Cody) that question, he was referring to Leo's
recently divorced sister, who didn't actually exist. But I answered

as if he were asking me about my *actual* mother, who really was doing well. Once aware of the duality, I began to acknowledge the privileges that come with having an alter ego.

You can learn a lot about yourself when you pretend to be someone else. Being Cody allowed me to participate in the world and yet still remain separate from it. I could hide behind his eyes and have interactions that weren't distorted by my own knowledge, my own insecurities, my own fears. In many ways, Cody's interactions were *more* honest and authentic than anything I was capable of. Because Cody *only* existed in that house. Which meant he had no expectations beyond whatever was happening at any given moment: He wasn't looking to make friends; he didn't care if a girl thought he was handsome; he didn't have an angle he was working to further his career. He didn't expect anything from anyone other than what he was receiving because he had no past or future. I was going to miss the freedom of living in those moments.

I was grateful (and surprised) to have made it that long without getting caught. Although one night things came close:

Three slackers showed up, each holding a brown paper bag. They were dressed so casually (torn jeans and stained T-shirts; one wore sweatpants!), Leo wanted to turn them away. But then they showed him the contents of their bags: Each sack contained a hundred thousand dollars in cash.

Right this way, gentlemen!

They were gamers. Internet dweebs during the peak of the online poker craze. These schlubs had made a fortune playing from the comfort of their mothers' basements.

Leo was thrilled. I had never seen him so excited. Before the game, he pulled me aside to say, "Listen, don't be afraid of these guys. They aren't gonna know what hit 'em!"

"Why? How do you know that?"

"They're e-donks," he said matter-of-factly.

"What the hell is an e-donk?"

"E-donks . . . you know . . . guys who only play online. They won't have an ounce of grift sense."

It all goes back to why Leo hired Ronnie in the first place. It used to be the case that very good poker players developed a "grift sense" over many thousands of hours in the card rooms. They became attuned to cheating techniques and methods, even if they weren't exactly experts in those moves themselves. But technology changed everything, on both sides of the game.

The average live poker game can run thirty hands an hour. It takes years to play 250,000 hands. When you fold, there's no choice but to sit and wait for the round to be finished before the next one starts. If you put in the time, round after round, day after day, month after month, assuming you were studious and intelligent, over the course of a decade you slowly became an expert poker player.

In the virtual world, a player can play multiple tables at the same time. Hundreds of hands an hour, upwards of 250,000 in a year. Which means a determined Internet player can, in just one year, have the same number of poker hands under his or her belt that took a legend like Doyle Brunson fifty years to accumulate.

This created an interesting phenomenon: Poker "experts" who had never actually played in live games. That meant they had never encountered any classic cheating techniques such as false shuffles, false deals, or marked cards. They understood the square game, but they were oblivious to the myriad ways the game could be rigged.

The e-donks didn't stand a chance.

Or so we thought. Imagine our surprise when, six hours into the game, after losing yet another hand, one of them, in disbelief, uttered the words: "That's not possible."

It turns out that playing thousands of hands at warp speed on the Internet may not help your grift sense, but it sure as hell helps develop an understanding of statistical probability. After losing too many consecutive hands to Leo, mathematical alarm bells sounded in the e-donk's head.

Luckily, they suspected Leo and not me. He was the one with the big pile of chips and the look of a shyster. They didn't know *how* he was winning, but the statistical anomaly was enough evidence to convince them he was doing "something."

A brief argument ensued. Leo defended his honor with an Oscar-worthy performance. He loved it, hamming it up and egging them on. Anything to keep them barking up the wrong tree. As long as they were pointing a finger at Leo, there was nothing that could be proven. Eventually the e-donks bagged up the money they had left and stormed out of the house. Leo laughed his ass off. Then he looked at me and said, "Oops."

Later that night, Leo joked, "Thank god Ronnie wasn't dealing or I'd be talking them out of calling the cops."

It took a beat for me to realize what he was saying: It's not that I was better than Ronnie. When it came to being a bust-out dealer, nobody was. After years of honing his craft, from ripping off drug dealers with dice in the alley to dealing for the Mob in Vegas, Ronnie was unstoppable at the table. But Ronnie had lived a hard life. You could hear it in the rasp of his voice; you could see it on his face, in his eyes, on his hands.

More to the point, Ronnie was black. Which meant he wasn't afforded any mistakes. If he was friendly, people thought he was "up to something." When he kept to himself, they wondered what he was hiding. If he was well dressed, they questioned where he'd gotten the money; when he dressed down, they asked who let him in the door. Perfect wasn't good enough.

I, on the other hand, was a clean-cut, baby-faced white guy. So, sadly, I could create an illusion of innocence that Ronnie never could. Leo understood this. Ronnie knew it better than anyone. Years earlier, he had told me, "Most of them thought I was guilty before I even touched the cards." Then he joked, "They happened to be right, but it's still fucked up."

Most nights weren't as eventful as the e-donk scare. I hesitate to imply that some nights were better than others, because that's like ranking the times I almost drowned. However, the "best" nights tended to be the evenings I dealt winning hands to the Honest Johns, the poker stars who were paid to play, unaware I was helping them win.

I met three in my time in that house: two World Series of Poker champs—guys I recognized from ESPN—and a gambler so legendary he was likened to "the king of gamblers," Nick the Greek. Dealing to these heavyweights didn't make my job easier, but it did make it more enjoyable because it was like having a celebrity at the table. In fact, it was better; we had quite a few celebrities come to the house and nobody cared. Not even a celebrity could distract from the action.

When a poker giant was there, the energy at the table was electric. It took some of the pressure off me and my hands. The superstars had the donks starstruck, like novice actors doing a scene with Meryl Streep. For the donks, it was a privilege to be with the Johns and an honor to lose to them.

I had so many questions for the Honest Johns. Especially the mysterious gambler whom Leo respectfully referred to as "Joe the Jew." (Apparently you're not an underground legend until you have "the" in your name.) He was a tiny man with an enormous presence and bushy eyebrows. I eavesdropped as Mr. Jew told the enamored donks his glory stories of winning millions, and the bad beats* that had taken it all back. He sounded like he was from the East Coast and used the word "mook" often. When he won hands he said, "Yatz!" which I loved because it reminded me of Ricky Jay, who said the same thing while throwing playing cards into watermelons. I wanted to ask Joe where that term came from, but I never got the chance. To him I was just another dealer. Why talk to the help when he could chat up his adoring fans at the table? I wonder what he would have said had he known I was helping him live up to his reputation. Now that Ronnie was coming back, I'd never get the chance to find out.

---

* *Bad beat*—a poker term for a hand in which a player with very strong cards loses to an opponent who is statistically unlikely to win, but hits a lucky card (or two) and unexpectedly takes the pot.

Then Leo said, "I have something I wanna run by you." Getting serious, he asked, "How would you feel about staying on after Ronnie gets out?"

I was flattered, but there was no way in hell I was taking Ronnie's gig. He was the reason I was there in the first place. When I told Leo as much, he corrected me: "You don't understand. I want you both to deal. Imagine what the two of you could do together."

I *had* imagined it. Had it been ten years earlier, I might not have hesitated to say yes. But things were different now. I told Leo I needed time to think about it. I wanted to discuss it with Vanessa. We were building a life together, and this wasn't a typical building block. This was supposed to be a temporary gig. I had my doubts she'd be happy living with a cheat. I had doubts I'd be happy living with myself.

At home, I made a list of pros and cons.

Seeing it in my journal now, it's humorous to me that I started with Cons. Not sure why I did that. Maybe I was nudging myself toward that decision. Regardless, having written so few words for each entry on the list, I'm forced to remember and speculate as to what I was thinking.

CON: Max. This is easy to decipher. I couldn't stand the guy. So much so that when I came up with reasons to stay or go, he was the very first thought I had. Continuing to work as a dealer meant putting up with him, and, even though his father sided with me virtually all the time, I wasn't sure that I could take it much longer. He was that awful and unpredictable.

PRO: Education. It's interesting, but not surprising, that this was the first Pro on the list. I had learned more about human behavior in those few months dealing than I had in all the years I'd lived up to that point. I had studied charlatans and cheats before, and how to manipulate perceptions, but this had been a graduate program in deception. And it wasn't just the flight time (the physical manipulation, the events at the table) that was so educational; it was having the ability to observe the donks, as if they were subjects in a grand experiment in which they didn't know they were participating. All that knowledge was practical. There was no place for theoretical deception in that house. Where else would I be given the opportunity to systematically deceive others, in the real world, again and again?

CON: Illegal. Hard to ignore this simple truth. It was illegal and, were I to get caught by the law, the trajectory of my life would change forever. Presumably not for the better.

PRO: $$$$. I was making money hand over fist. In fact, I was bringing home so much cash, we were running out of places to hide it in our small apartment. Behind the books on the bookshelves, in pots we never used in the kitchen, in Vanessa's shoeboxes. With a pitiful résumé and no college degree, there was no way in hell I was going to find a job that paid as well.

Plenty of people proclaim that "money can't buy happiness." But having money certainly seemed to make it *easier* to be happy. I had no idea how much of my mind had been consumed by money—not having any—until I had some. Now, instead of worrying about taking my car to the mechanic because the CHECK ENGINE light was on, I just bought a new car. We had paid off our credit cards and were well on our way to saving for our future.

And I remembered what it was like standing in a circle with Vanessa's Ivy League coworkers. How inadequate I felt as they compared their Rolexes. It was the same feeling of *less than* that I had at the Broadmoor with Walt. Then I contrasted that to my experience when I'd attended another event with many of the same faces, during my time as a dealer. I felt different; the fancy people with shiny things didn't intimidate me. I wasn't embarrassed by my lack of education or proletariat roots. When they discussed watches, instead of feeling inferior, I felt sorry for them—sorry that they coveted such things, sorry that they had nothing of real value to discuss. Perhaps the only reason I could hold my head high in the circle I once feared was the fact that I was making more money than Vanessa's boss. Standing with the handsome businessmen, I could have afforded a Rolex. And, at that time in my life, knowing I *could* made all the difference.

CON: Dangerous. Although I hadn't been caught, I never lost sight of the fact that it wasn't the safest line of work. I couldn't let my guard down or get complacent. The smallest slip could be my last.

PRO: Sky is the limit! That's something Leo said to me. After spending time with me, he started to recognize that I was more than just a pretty set of hands. He told me, "The rest of the world is just like that card table. If you can learn to see that, with your talent, the sky's the limit."

Dealing gave me a chance to recognize *my* value. The esoteric skills and arcane knowledge I had acquired were deemed trivial by the outside world. But as a bust-out dealer, my talents had a utility. What I could do mattered. I mattered. Leo helped me see that.

Leo wasn't a sleight-of-hand artist like Ronnie or a conjuring scholar like Walt; he was a different kind of deceiver. And he didn't think that my craft should be limited to a stage or card table. He was more generous with his praise than Walt or Ronnie, who both had a tough-love approach to mentoring me. Leo helped me build confidence, and he encouraged me. It seemed like, for the first time, I might have found a mentor who aligned with my ambitions. I felt there was much I could learn from Leo. And with his guidance, who knows how far I could go.

CON: V/Social life. The *V* was for "Vanessa." Working as a dealer had taken a significant toll on my relationship with her and on our social life. While I only worked one or two nights a week, my sleep schedule had permanently shifted. I went to bed around the time she woke up. We had become ships passing in the night.

She also worried that I would fall into the lifestyle that dominated Leo's house. Understandably so. I had made the mistake of telling her about the seedy clientele, their drug habits and their philandering, and how Max regularly brought strippers to the house. I can only imagine the dark fantasies that played out in Vanessa's mind. So I tried to keep it light, mostly telling her about the more pleasant and humorous events. But even the most lighthearted answer to the question "How was your night at work?" was tainted with inescapable subtext: *So I was sitting there stealing money from strangers . . .*

Also, we were both only children from broken homes, so our friends were our families and we loved them dearly. But when I started working as a dealer, we saw them less and less for one simple reason: I couldn't lie to them. I wouldn't lie to them. So I avoided them, as if that were somehow better.

PRO: Freedom. I think I was referring to the independence I had as a dealer. I had plenty of time to do other things. (I didn't do other things, but I could've.) I didn't really have a boss, which was a first. Leo hired me, but he treated me less like an employee and more like the star in his theatrical production. Eddie *thought* he was my boss, but he wasn't. Any time he pissed me off or tried to make my life more difficult, I just went to Leo and it was taken care of. Eventually Eddie realized it was easier to leave me be and wrote it off as favoritism. After all, I was Leo's nephew. It was unlikely that I'd find another line of work that would allow me so much autonomy.

CON: Secrets. I was so damn tired of carrying secrets.

Perhaps that's yet another reason I was drawn to Leo. Deception seemed effortless for him; he seemed unburdened by it all. I, too, wanted to be free from all the things I was hiding. *Is it possible to do both? Can you hold a secret without carrying its weight?*

The tally was Cons: 5, Pros: 4.

Notably absent from the Cons column was any consideration of morality or ethics. I knew that it was wrong, intellectually. But it didn't *feel* wrong. That's probably because my reason for being there was righteous and just: *I am helping a friend (who has cancer!) keep his job.*

That felt like a solid justification for doing a questionable thing. But, with only two games remaining, that excuse was about to expire. My mission to keep the game going was nearly accomplished. After Ronnie returned, if I were to agree to keep dealing, there could be no denying that I was there for me.

It's pretty clear to me now that the Cons and Pros list was a bit of intellectual theater I was performing for myself. I wanted to convince myself that I was *trying* to make the right decision. I wanted to prove that, at the very least, I was being sensible. I wanted to *believe* that it was a hard decision so I could believe I was a good person.

I called Leo and accepted his offer, agreeing to continue dealing after Ronnie returned.

IN THE LIGHT OF THE DARK

It happened relatively early, before midnight. Thankfully, Max was off doing god knows what, so the room was quiet, peaceful. Without an Honest John, Leo was set to be the big winner for the night. There were four donks at the table; including Jerry, whose face looked sad even when he smiled, seated to my right.

Jerry had been to the game three or four times since I had been dealing. He was soft-spoken and polite. I never saw him flirt with a waitress, never heard him curse. Compared with the other donks, he seemed like a decent fellow. Every time I saw him I was certain it'd be the last, because he didn't look like he could afford to be there. Despite looking broke, he always tipped the staff, including me. Every time he played, he set a few chips aside to make sure he had ten or twenty to toss my way.

He was the first person to tip me at the table and I rejected it, saying, "Oh, that's not necessary."

Later, when we were alone, Leo gave me an earful. "What the hell are you doing rejecting tips?!"

"I just beat the guy for everything and I'm supposed to let him tip me for it?!"

"Yes! All the dealers accept tips. You turn down money and people are gonna wake up. Next time someone gives you a tip, take it!"

I didn't make that mistake again.

Things were different the last night I saw Jerry. As usual, he went all in on a hand that he was destined to lose. But this time he forgot to set a few chips aside for tips. I, of course, was fine with that. But Jerry wasn't. So he reached into his pocket and, after scrounging for a moment, emerged with the only cash he had left: a crumpled five-dollar bill.

There's an old gambler's saying: *Whoever invented gambling was smart, but the inventor of chips was a genius.*

Poker chips allow you to lose sight of the fact that you're wagering money. Money is sacred and vital, but colorful disks are fun and playful. If you saw a five-dollar bill in the middle of a quiet street, you'd certainly pick it up. If it were a little blue chip, it wouldn't be worth your time. I believe that has something to do with what came next.

Jerry smoothed out some of the creases on the five-dollar bill before presenting it to me, saying, "Sorry, dealer, I wish it was more."

The moment the bill hit the table, a blinding white light

instantly filled the room. In a flash, the walls and ceiling evaporated. All I could see were my hands, until they, too, were consumed by the hot white light. Nothing remained, not even me; only light.

After a moment of calm and silence, the light suddenly retreated from every corner of the room. As if someone hit the Rewind button on the Big Bang, the white light was sucked back into the single point from which it first appeared, back into the center of the five-dollar bill.

The room went black. And still. Absolute silence. Without anything to see or hear, I was forced to take notice of how I felt, which was ice-cold. Winter-night-in-the-Rocky-Mountains cold. Then the silence was breached by a crackling sound. A dim, fiery glow slowly illuminated the room. My eyes adjusted to the low light. The first thing I saw was my own breath.

There were no blue walls or white ceiling. I was in a cavernous space, walls and ceiling made of solid earth. I was still seated, but not behind the wood-and-green-felt poker table. It was now a large slab of rock. On it, there were no cards made of plastic or colorful chips, no dealer button or drinks. In place of those objects were impossibly perfect shadows.

But these shadows weren't flattened to the surface as shadows should be. They were bits of dark fog sculpted to resemble real objects. There were no objects to cast these shadows. The shadows themselves were the objects.

Only one real, familiar object remained on the table: the five-dollar bill with Lincoln's wrinkled green face staring up at me. The man who had left it was gone, but three other donks remained. And, like the rest of my surroundings, they, too, looked different.

The donks had chains around their bodies and shackles around their necks. They were prisoners. Leo, however, had no chains or shackles. The only thing different about him was the cigar in his hand. It had been replaced by a shadow, the exact size and shape, with a fiery ember at its tip.

I heard the clicking and clacking of poker chips. One of the prisoners was sorting a stack of shadows as if they were chips. Then I heard ice cubes clink against glass as another prisoner took a sip from his dark, fog-like drink.

This can't be happening.

I looked at Leo, bewildered and scared. He smiled and took a puff off his cigar-shaped shadow, then nodded, pointing my attention back to the five-dollar bill.

Is he seeing what I'm seeing?

I reached for the bill, but the moment my hand touched the five, its color began to fade as it transformed into a shadow. Lincoln's face dissolved first. Then the numbers, down to the very last words IN GOD WE TRUST, until they were gone, too, and all that remained was a shadow of the same size and shape.

How is this possible?

I felt the same sensation I had when Walt first transformed and vanished his pocketknife. The absence of all knowledge washed over me. Only this time there was no trick. At least not one I could decipher. I was even more confounded when I realized the bill-shaped shadow in my hand still felt like paper.

Suddenly I heard, "Let's go, dealer!"

I looked up to see the prisoners waiting expectantly for their game to resume. But there was no game. There were no cards to deal or chips to bet, only shadows. Leo gave me a nod, encouraging me to continue. I was so lost.

Afraid to upset the table, I placed the shadow that was once a five-dollar bill aside and grabbed the shadow that resembled a deck of cards. That shadow consisted of thinner shadows, which I shuffled. I dealt two shadows to each of the players. They looked at their shadows as if they were cards.

Have you ever seen a child play with a doll when they think no one is watching? Their eyes reflect another world, one quite different from yours. But it's clear from their sincerity that whatever world they are inhabiting at that moment, to them, is no less real than yours.

That's how these prisoners looked while staring at their shadows. It was as if everyone else at the table was experiencing a collective hallucination, seeing something I couldn't see. It reminded me of church, when everyone closed their eyes to see the same lovely thing, and no matter how hard I tried, I couldn't see what they saw.

Growing up, we're taught the danger of having an imagination so vivid we forget the world itself. We learn the hazards of getting lost in a land of make-believe: *It's okay to venture in, just not too far, and never for too long, or risk finding yourself in an even more perilous place: belief.*

I tried to blink my way back to reality, but it didn't work. This was my new reality. I began to feel trapped. It was cold and dark, and I didn't want to be there anymore. Panic set in. I could see my breaths getting shorter. The moment was reminiscent of the time I woke up trapped inside my own body, enveloped by darkness. Only this time, my eyes were wide open.

Suddenly I remembered the key to my freedom that day in my bed—it was acceptance. So I closed my eyes and submitted to the darkness around me. The sounds in the room faded to absolute silence.

Then a muffled voice began repeating the same thing over and over again, louder and louder, until I clearly heard that it was Leo saying, "Cody. Cody. Cody!"

My eyes sprung open. The walls were blue, the ceiling was white. I was back behind the poker table full of colorful chips. The donks, no longer in chains and shackles, were once again holding cards instead of shadows, and they were staring at me as if I were crazy.

Leo looked concerned, too. "You okay?" he asked.

I didn't know *what* I was. At the very least, I was shaken and bewildered. I wanted to tell them all what I had just seen. Like Dorothy returning from Oz. *And you and you and you . . . and you were there.*

I simply muttered, "I'm okay," and apologized for "spacing out." Then I quickly assessed the action on the table and resumed dealing. I told myself to breathe, trying to calm myself down. I told myself it was just a daydream or hallucination. But the longer I sat there, the more difficult it became to deny the truth. It felt like I had seen a secret I wasn't meant to see. Like seeing the little red ball hiding in the magician's hand. The illusion I was living in had been destroyed. The real world now felt—there's no other way to describe it—*less real.*

I wanted to tell the donks what I had witnessed, but I remembered how the Allegory of the Cave ended, with accusations of madness and threats of violence. So I said nothing. And I watched the donks look at their cards just as they had looked at the shadows, knowing they were one and the same.

I had given myself too much credit. I thought that the donks were losing because I was the one rigging the game. But it never was a game; it was a *simulation* of a game. And not just when I was dealing. Even the legitimate moments of gambling, when the cards were really shuffled and fairly dealt, were in service of a fantasy set in the real world; an elaborate story so convincing, its characters didn't even know they were living lives authored by someone else. And, as is true with most works of theater, it was the characters that brought the story to life.

With the exception of Leo, Max, and me, the rest of the cast was completely unaware of the plot. As far as the staff knew, they were just doing their jobs. And that's what made them so believable. Real dealers were hired to portray dealers, bartenders were hired to pour drinks, the chef cooked delicious meals, and the servers served it all. My employer even managed to get a real LAPD officer to play the part of off-duty cop who guards the game. These unknowing actors were oblivious to the story they were telling and completely ignorant of this crucial fact: Their truths were in service of a lie.

The most convincing characters were the donks themselves.

Over and over again, I watched them validate one another's belief that what they were experiencing was real. And to them it *was* real. They believed, with every fiber of their beings, that they were poker players, playing poker. They were as certain of their reality as you are of yours right now.

I had thought that the only thing I was taking from them was their money. But after seeing them in their chains, it was painfully clear to me that theft was the lesser of two crimes. They weren't poker players. They were prisoners, trapped by an illusion, unable to escape because they believed they were already free.

I continued dealing (without cheating) as I tried to come to grips with it all. Two or three more hands were dealt before I noticed Leo squirming in his seat. It had been a while since he had won, and he was growing impatient because I hadn't been doing my job.

I wanted to be a good soldier and give Leo a win. *Come on, man! Pull yourself together!* But the moment I considered cheating, my hands filled with that arctic chill, just as they had on my first night, something that hadn't occurred in weeks, possibly months.

Ignore it. You've fought through it before, you can do it again!

I started shuffling with nefarious intent and the freeze intensified. Then, as I continued to shuffle, something new occurred: The frost in my hands broke through the creases of my wrists. It was a boundary the ice had never crossed before. The chill flowed through my veins and up my arms. I felt it hit my shoulders and chest. It entered my heart, where it stayed for a moment, then it abruptly spread to every corner of my body. My entire body was freezing. And it was now impossible to ignore the fact: It was the same crisp chill I had felt when I found myself in the cave.

I abandoned any notion of cheating and dealt on the square. Leo continued to get visibly frustrated as he was forced to fold hand after hand after hand. For the first time, I didn't care. It didn't matter if he was mad or if I was letting him down. I wasn't doing it for him. I wasn't even doing it for Ronnie now.

Koko, the other dealer, returned to relieve me. Leo looked angry, and I knew he wouldn't wait long to confront me. So I grabbed my tray, half-full of chips, and, instead of taking my usual dinner break, I marched straight to Eddie's office.

I was only halfway through that night. And there was still another night of dealing before Ronnie returned. But I knew I couldn't deal *another* hand. Not one more. As far as I was concerned, I had made good on my promise to Ronnie. If quitting *one* night early meant the operation came crashing down, so be it. I was done.

Eddie was leaning back in his chair behind his desk, his legs kicked up onto the desktop, with an outdated laptop on his lap. I set my tray on his desk. "What's this?" he asked as I turned to walk away. "Hey, where you going?" I ignored him. Then, "Cody!" as if he were talking to a dog. "Get your ass back here, boy!"

I stopped to remove my name tag. Tossing it on his desk, I said, "That's not my name."

Then I walked out of his office and the house, forever.

At home, I confided in Vanessa, telling her I was done dealing.

I thanked her for her patience and love. As much as I wanted to tell her about the cave, I didn't. I couldn't, it sounded insane. I decided she didn't need to know *how* I'd come to quit. She just had to know that I was never going back.

She told me she was glad to have me home. And she surprised me with her final comment: "I hope you found what you were looking for."

Leo called me nonstop that night, but I never answered. He called more over the next several days. I deleted his messages without listening to them. Then I started getting calls from UNKNOWN CALLER. I didn't pick up. If there was one thing Leo was good at, it was getting people to do things they didn't want to do. I had made up my mind, but I didn't want to risk being seduced back into his world. So I avoided his calls as if they were songs of the Sirens.

I began to notice a black car with tinted windows outside my apartment. It would be there and then it wouldn't be there. Could it have been there for me? Could it have just been a car that happened to park on my street that week, and only that week? I never found out.

Two weeks later I got a text message from a number I didn't recognize, but the message read: *Hey, it's Ronnie. Hit me back.* I texted back: *Call me when you're alone.*

When I answered his call, he said, "Where you at, little brother!" It was good to hear his voice. He sounded free. But he also sounded softer. His chemo treatments had been taking a toll on him.

"I was worried about you," he said. Leo told him I had vanished and that he couldn't get ahold of me. I told Ronnie I was fine, but made it clear that my days of dealing were behind me.

Concerned I may have been wronged, Ronnie got serious, asking, "Did something happen?"

I told him it was nothing like that, reassured him that I was fine, then quickly changed the subject. I asked Ronnie what he was up to.

"Getting ready to go back to work, thanks to you!" he said. Ronnie went on to profusely thank me for keeping his seat warm for him. I said, "No problem," and then asked him about his health. He lied and told me he was fine.

I couldn't help but wonder where I stood with Leo. I hadn't expected to leave the way I did. And even though I'd stormed out, I wasn't sure I wanted to completely sever ties with him. I had so many questions. For all I knew, Leo was the only person who could answer them.

I asked Ronnie, "Is Leo upset?"

"Nah, I think he was just worried about you."

"Tell Leo I'm fine and thank him for the opportunity."

"Will do! Maybe you come by and visit us sometime. It'd be great to see ya," he said.

"I'll try," I told him, knowing I would never go back to that house. But I sincerely added, "It'd be great to see you, too."

I wanted to ask Ronnie about the cave, if he had seen it, what he knew. But I didn't. I was afraid to hear his answer.

THE DIFFERENCE

It had been nearly a year since the cave had revealed itself to me. The money I made casting shadows provided me with some financial breathing room. Vanessa was able to quit one of her jobs and, living below our means, I didn't feel obligated to take the first job I was offered. Instead of getting a steady gig, I began studying art and politics, working with an artist named Glenn.

Long before his work was in museums, Glenn was tagging walls and getting into fistfights with rival LA gangs. His art studio was only a few blocks from my apartment. Just as I had struck a deal with Walt at the magic shop, Glenn and I came to an arrangement: I'd share what I knew about illusions (all matters of deception and secrecy). In return, Glenn would allow me access to his studio (which was as close to a Wonka Factory as I had ever seen) and his private library, and offer his guidance and wisdom (of which he had plenty).

I went to his studio every day and read about magicians I had never heard of: Duchamp. Kosuth. Abramović. Huyghe. Debord. Burden. Beuys. There I learned about (and participated in) a wide array of production processes with various forms of art-making. There I focused on revealing more than I concealed. Slowly but surely, I was learning how to make the invisible visible.

I was at that studio when Ronnie called. I didn't even recognize his voice at first, he sounded so meek. It had been nearly a

year since our last phone call and he said he just wanted to hear my voice. I felt guilty for having gone so long without calling to check on him, but I was happy he called.

I asked him if he was still dealing for Leo. He said, "Nah, that shit ended months ago," and quickly changed the subject, asking me, "So how are you and the angel doing?"

After briefly catching up, he said, "I wanted to let you know I'm coming to town for a day. It'd be great to see you."

When I asked him why he was coming to town he replied, "I just gotta do a thing." It was uncharacteristically cryptic; he was always blunt and forthcoming with me. I didn't need to press too hard to get the truth. He was coming to LA to see a doctor, a cancer specialist at Ronald Reagan UCLA Medical Center. A friend of a friend had given him a referral and he got an appointment. All he had to do was make the trip from Vegas.

He broke down his schedule: "I'm getting in early afternoon. I do the thing. I'm free for a bit. Then I drive back later that night. In and out."

"Why don't you crash at our place for the night? Vanessa would love to see you."

"Thanks but I gotta get back, I got stuff to do here."

I didn't like the idea of him driving back late at night. That stretch of desert is long and dark, easy to doze off behind the wheel. He assured me that he'd made the trip hundreds of times and he'd be fine. Normally I would have believed him, but it didn't sound right to me.

I couldn't convince him to stay the night. And there was no way he was getting on a plane. So I did the only other thing I could think of doing: I flew to Vegas to drive him to his appointment and back.

I saw him as I was getting out of my taxi in front of his apartment building. He had lost a great deal of weight and patches of his hair, but he was still himself. He didn't want me to see him appearing less than vibrant. But he was grateful I had come to help. He hugged me with tears in his eyes.

The journey was only four or five hours each way, but we stocked up on snacks as if we were driving to Knoxville. I drove his white Cadillac so he could relax while he told me the story of why he was no longer dealing for Leo.

"It wasn't what it seemed, man." He said this reluctantly and with a heavy sigh.

"You saw the cave?" I asked, excited to finally have someone to confide in.

"The what? No. What's that?"

"Oh, nothing," I said, hiding my disappointment, then pressed on. "What happened?!"

I wasn't prepared for his answer.

"Remember how Max was always fucking up and losing?"

"Yeah?" I had no idea where this was going.

"He was doing it on purpose."

I calmly pulled the car over and turned the radio off. "What?"

There, on the shoulder of Interstate 15, surrounded by the Mojave Desert, Ronnie proceeded to blow my mind.

All of those nights that Max recklessly lost the money I had cheated to send his way, he was *intentionally* dumping chips to a confederate whom Leo had secretly hired to sit in and play. Leo did this because we, the bust-out dealers, were paid based on the percentage of the take. So, by having Max "lose" much of his money to this secret player, they didn't have to pay us as much at the end of the night.

"Leo was paying guys five hundred bucks and a steak dinner to fuck us over," Ronnie explained.

"How'd you figure it out?" I asked.

"That dumbass [Leo] called one of my friends to sit in. My man hung up and called me, saying, 'Yo, I think your boss just asked me to fuck you over.'" Then Ronnie added, "Needless to say, I didn't go back."

I sat there stunned, grappling with the new information. All that time I was dealing to the donks, I was the prisoner of a *cave within a cave*. Like the donks, I was unable to escape because I believed I was already free.

Then a thought hit me like a sledgehammer: Max, the fuckup. All his impulsive, reckless behavior. His showboating and bravado. The stupidity. It was all a performance. And it wasn't for the donks. It was for me.

I asked, "So those arguments Leo and Max got into, that was all an act?"

"Fuck . . ." Ronnie said, shaking his head. "I don't even think they were father and son."

We were parked safely on the side of the road but it felt as though I had just experienced a violent collision. I sat there silently coping with the pain and assessing the wreckage of a truth.

"Whatever, fuck those guys," Ronnie said, ready to move

on. He'd learned this information months ago. And, sadly, he'd grown to expect betrayal and injustice. I pulled myself together enough to get back on the road. Had I not needed to get Ronnie to his appointment I might still be there on the side of the road, contemplating what I had just learned.

We continued dissecting the ruse. By the time we reached Barstow, the feeling of betrayal had been paired with a sense of astonishment. I really had to hand it to Leo and Max—which I now doubted were their real names. They put on a hell of a show and played their parts to perfection.

I realized, even though Max was an insufferable prick to me, it was Leo who was truly cruel. All those talks he and I had. The advice he gave me. All the pats on the back. Every time he told me he was proud of me. It was all fiction. And I believed it. Because I wanted to. Leo recognized that. He knew *exactly* what story I was telling myself. And he knew long before I did.

I grew up knowing children are born loved by a mother and father. Which meant as long as I didn't have a father, I'd only ever be half loved. I didn't choose to believe that narrative. It was inevitable. How could I not believe the only thing I ever knew?

My father's absence was a sign that read: 20 MILES TO JOP-LIN. Leo saw it and immediately knew how to exploit it. That's why he treated me like a son.

What kind of person would do such a thing?

I knew the answer. I was *becoming* the answer. The void that Leo exploited was composed of the same dark matter I saw at that table. Had the cave not revealed itself, I might have stayed and continued chasing the shadow of a father.

At the doctor's office, Ronnie had his checkup and I sat alone in the waiting room, stewing in my own thoughts. I was still dwelling on the past during dinner with Ronnie at his favorite Mexican restaurant. It wasn't until we hit the road back to Vegas later that night that I was able to start thinking about the future.

"So what's next for you?" Ronnie asked.

"I have no idea."

Then Ronnie surprised me, saying, "You know what I always saw you doing someday?"

"What's that?"

"Writing."

"Really?" I said. "Why?" He had never seen anything I had written because, other than scribbles in my notebook, I had never written anything.

"I don't know. I like the way you tell stories."

It was as high a compliment as I'd ever receive.

"I wouldn't even know where to begin," I said.

"Just pick a story and start writing."

I already knew what story I wanted to tell. I just didn't know how to tell it. Also, writing about the cave meant writing about my time in that house, and I wasn't sure if I could do that. Testing the waters, I said, "Maybe I should write about dealing."

"Hell yeah, you should do that."

"Really?" I said.

"Of course! People love hearing about other people getting fucked over."

Not exactly what I had in mind, but true.

Then I asked, "What about Leo and Max?"

"Man, fuck those guys. Can't wait to read it."

"Okay, then!" I said, excited by the fantasy of writing.

We arrived at Ronnie's apartment while it was still dark out. But we continued talking until the sun came up. Ronnie fell asleep in his recliner and I crashed on his couch for a few hours. Then, as Ronnie was sleeping like a baby, I quietly let myself out and headed to the airport to catch my flight home.

Had I known that was the last time I would ever see Ronnie, I would have woken him up to say goodbye. The treatments didn't work. Ronnie lost his battle to cancer later that same year. At his funeral, an old-timer in attendance remarked that it was the most impressive gathering of charlatans and swindlers since the death of Titanic Thompson.

At the airport in Vegas, still invigorated by my conversation with Ronnie and determined to get started, I bought a new notebook at a kiosk. I wanted to dive right in and write about the cave, but decided I should ease into it. For inspiration, I looked back at what I didn't know would be my last conversation with Ronnie.

Before we fell asleep in his living room, Ronnie asked, "Did I tell you what happened before I found out Leo was a lying piece a shit?"

"No, what's that?"

Ronnie proceeded to tell me a remarkable story: He told me about beating a donk, an Armenian "with a bad habit of scratching the stubble on the side of his head whenever he held a decent hand." After losing all his money, the Armenian produced a snub-nosed revolver and the table went dead quiet.

"I thought I was a goner," Ronnie said, reliving the trauma. "But then the dude set it on the table and said, 'How much can I get for this?'"

Leo bought the gun off the Armenian for four hundred dollars in chips. Ronnie took that money back the very next hand.

"You know what?" he said, perking up a little. "You should put that in your book."

"Really?"

"Hell yeah. Just don't mention me. In fact, say it happened to you."

"But it didn't," I said.

He replied, "They'll never know the difference."

ACKNOWLEDGMENTS

Many thanks to Vanessa Lauren, Alexandra DelGaudio, Jennifer Lohrig, Jason England, Joy Ivey, Glenn Kaino, Jake Friedman, Michael Weber, Frank Oz, Victoria Labalme, Enrique Enriquez, Jared Kopf, Adam Rubin, Robert Herritt, Tom Werner, Neil Patrick Harris, Evelyn McGee Colbert, Stephen Colbert, Laurie Eustis, Oskar Eustis, Neil Gaiman, Tom Hanks, Jelani Cobb, Paul Holdengräber, Mike Pisciotta, Mark Modeer, Jessica Modeer, Ed Andres, Kate Rachwitz, Eric Suddleson, Neal Brennan, Peter Gethers, Tatiana Dubin, Reagan Arthur, Sloan Harris, Michael R. Fleming, Sebastian Clergue, Brendan Walter, Riki Blanco, Ximena Feijoo Merklen, Luis Piedrahita, Ricky Jay, Steve Forte, R.D., B.M., A.M., N.J.G., and the Shadow Boys.

Derek DelGaudio is a writer and performer, primarily known for creating his highly acclaimed theater show, *In & Of Itself*. He served as the Artist-in-Residence for Walt Disney Imagineering and cofounded the performance art collective A.BANDIT. Mr. DelGaudio lives in New York City.

A NOTE ON THE TYPE

This book was set in Janson, a typeface named for the Dutch-man Anton Janson, but is actually the work of Nicholas Kis (1650–1702). The type is an excellent example of the influential and sturdy Dutch types that prevailed in England up to the time William Caslon (1692–1766) developed his own incomparable designs from them.

Typeset by Scribe, Philadelphia, Pennsylvania

Printed and bound by Friesens, Altona, Manitoba

Designed by Anna B. Knighton